MW100860743

Localism

LOCALISM

Coming Home to
Catholic Social Teaching

Edited by Dale Ahlquist
and Michael Warren Davis

SOPHIA INSTITUTE PRESS
Manchester, New Hampshire

Sophia Institute Press
Box 5284, Manchester, NH 03108
1-800-888-9344
www.SophiaInstitute.com

Sophia Institute Press® is a registered trademark of Sophia Institute.

hardcover ISBN 979-8-88911-304-1

ebook ISBN 979-8-88911-305-8

Library of Congress Control Number: 2024932567

First printing

Contents

A New Name for Distributism

DALE AHLQUIST

*Like all sane men and most mad ones
I am concerned about social reform.*

—G. K. Chesterton

One hundred years ago, when G. K. Chesterton and Hilaire Belloc and their colleagues formed a league to promote the idea of widespread property ownership and independence, they kept trying to come up with a name to call themselves other than "The League." Chesterton suggested "The League of Little People," but it was deemed too paradoxical. Belloc hit on the term "Distributivism" (though some would describe it as a miss rather than a hit) to describe their philosophy, and they soon started calling themselves "The Distributist League," but nobody liked it. The term was misunderstood immediately, and then it disintegrated from there.

Fast forward some sixty years to the beginning of a revival of interest in Chesterton and Belloc. Along with it came a renewed

Localism

interest in distributism. And also a renewed dislike of the name distributism. But the happy few who grasped the idea were unsatisfied with any term that did not completely explain the idea — even though "distributism" didn't explain it either.

The word "distributism" does not suggest property or small business or self-government or family or freedom; it does, however, lend itself to being confused with re-distribution, which is what taxation is. Micro-minded capitalists considered us socialists, while bubble-brained socialists feared we were fascists.

Distributism aims to be the application of Catholic Social Teaching, which was first promulgated by Pope Leo XIII in his 1891 encyclical *Rerum Novarum* and was reaffirmed if not expounded on by all the popes ever since, especially Pope Pius XI in *Quadragesimo Anno*. It is based on the idea that "more workers should become owners" and that widespread ownership would provide freedom and independence and make for a more just society. It did not pull any punches, claiming that industrial capitalism is responsible for many grave ills in modern society and that socialism is the well-intentioned but wrong-headed solution that only makes matters worse.

Distributism is opposed to centralization, whether it be political or commercial. It is about directness. It is about dignity. It is about responsibility, which is the flip side of freedom. It puts the family's rights above the individual or the community, but in recognizing the family as primary, it serves both the individual and the community, that is, the common good.

The Society of Gilbert Keith Chesterton, in its role of promoting all of G. K. Chesterton's writings and ideas, was finally tired of trying explain and spread the idea of distributism under the burden of its cumbersome and confusing name. We were not trying to change the idea. We were not trying to change the philosophy. We were trying to introduce a better word – better in that it had an immediate, recognizable meaning and, for the most part, an immediate appeal. It was not a perfect term, and it certainly did not encompass the entire idea, but it had great virtue, and we started using it: localism.

It is a word that already has a meaning: the support of local production and consumption of goods, local control of government, the promotion of local history, local culture, and local identity, and the protection of local freedom. It obviously favors directness and decentralization, and it is even more obviously opposed to globalism and collectivism.

Normal people want to take responsibility for their own lives, and they are increasingly frustrated and alienated by the fact that everything is out of their control and they cannot really say who *is* in control. They are weary of the complexities and complications brought on by bottomless bureaucracy and endless regulations, everything separated from everything else, and no one being answerable for anything.

Localism means having a say in what happens to you. It means keeping accountable those who have power that affects you. As Chesterton says, you should be able to keep your politicians close enough to be able to kick them. It means keeping your dollars in your community, buying from your neighbor, and thereby supporting your neighbor. It means owning your own piece of the community. It means being your own boss.

And as for local, there is nothing more local than the family. There is nothing more local than the home. By localism, we mean an economy and a political system based on the family. When Christ came, He first came into a family. Chesterton says Christianity has always been a domestic religion because it started with the Holy Family. And he says that each family is a tiny kingdom – that is, a local kingdom – the only state that creates and loves its own citizens.

Localism

If we begin with the dignity of providing for and protecting and loving our own families, the next natural step is to treat our neighbors with the same respect and charity so that their families can enjoy what we enjoy. Thus, Catholic Social Teaching – and localism – may be summed up as "Love your neighbor as yourself." Chesterton says:

> The truth has made us free; the tradition has given to men the sort of liberty they really like; local customs, individual craftsmanship, variety of self-expression, the presence of personality in production, the dignity of the human will. These are expressed in a thousand things, from hospitality to adventure, from parents instructing their own children to children inventing their own games, from practical jokes to pilgrimages and from patron saints to pub signs. (*G. K.'s Weekly*, June 12, 1926)

It all sounds great. But what are the problems with it, other than the fact that everyone thinks there is only capitalism or communism to choose from, a choice reinforced by the institutional might of university economics departments, well-funded think tanks, and oppressive state regimes?

It was once normal to live on a farm. Then it was normal to at least be related to someone who lived on a farm. When that stopped being normal, so did everything else. Cities, those exceptions on the landscape, became more and more disconnected from the land. Then came the suburbs, where life was neither this nor that. G. K. Chesterton describes Hell as the place where nothing happens. It is a good description of the suburbs. While people "live" in the suburbs, they usually work somewhere else and spend most of their time and money somewhere else. They don't know their neighbors, they don't enjoy a sense of local community, and they don't care about city government except to complain about it. The suburbs are served by remotely owned chain stores, so there is no local economy. I have traveled all around the country, and as soon as I reach the outskirts of any downtown, a set of sameness sets in. I could be anywhere. Every place looks like every other place. Add to that the suburban schools. They are also the same everywhere, built to look and function like state correctional facilities.

So the first challenge facing localism is the suburbs. That's where the change has to happen first. People have to start taking back their zip codes. One immediate way to do that is to start your own school. Start giving your money to locally owned businesses. Start being a locally owned business. Start being a voice in local government. Can it happen? G. K. Chesterton, who is right about most things, says yes:

> It often happens in history that things intensely small and local, or even backward and barbaric, defend themselves with great success against empires and combines, simply because they are too remote to have been overawed by mere cosmopolitan rumour and reputation. There are some fortunate communities that are too ignorant to be bullied, too superstitious to be frightened, too poor to be bribed, and too small to be destroyed. It is probably in these minute and secret places that the seed of civilization will be preserved for future ages, through the blundering anarchy of big things which seems to be coming upon us. (*G. K.'s Weekly*, July 21, 1928)

How to Get Back to the Land

MAX BECHER

Aspiring Back-to-the-Landers are sprouting almost as quickly as the grass between my corn rows. Far from being weeds, though, would-be homesteaders should be carefully cultivated to "preserve for the nation the essential elements of what might be called genuine rural culture." These words of Pope Pius XII to Italian farmers in his 1946 *Allocution to Italian Farmers* are ever more urgent today, as "the moral recovery of our whole people depends on a class of farmers socially sound and religiously firm."

Eight decades later, Catholics across America, particularly youth and young families, are rediscovering the agrarian side of Catholic Social Teaching as they grow weary of consumerism's empty promises. But for this impetus to become an impactful lay movement, more is needed than hope, right principles, and good intentions. This movement demands significant shifts in lifestyle and requires practical knowledge, skills, and relentless determination. The homesteader who crosses the threshold from theory to action must spend more time with his hands on the hoe, kneading bread, or inside a birthing animal, than reading G. K. Chesterton, Wendell Berry, and essays such as this. Lest Catholic agrarianism stagnate as an intellectual sport, the homesteader-hopeful must understand the essence of what he is aiming for, the best way to get there, and mistakes to avoid on the way. He also must be encouraged to take the first steps, confident that this way of life is not only possible but immensely rewarding. Society and the Church desperately need more homesteading families.

First and foremost, if the land calls your heart, start with the end in mind, and use it as your measure of success. As Catholics, we know we have been called to be fruitful and multiply and to direct all life toward the Kingdom of God. We also know this vocation is carried out primarily through the family, the vital cell of society. "As the family goes, so goes the nation."

For this reason, the Catholic authors of the 1939 *Manifesto on Rural Life* note in the opening paragraphs, "the special adaptability of the farm home for nurturing strong and wholesome Christian family life is the primary reason why the Catholic Church is so deeply concerned with rural problems.... The farm is the native habitat of the family." Pius XII tells farmers that "Your being so strongly rooted in the family constitutes the importance of your contribution to the correct development of the private and public order of society."

The family homestead and agrarian lifestyle are uniquely suited to wholesome Christian family life, which in turn builds up society and the Church. The Church champions the farm for the sake of the family. Rule number one for budding Catholic homesteaders: if the homestead is causing undue stress on your family, you are doing something wrong or moving too fast. Take the time to figure out which one, if not both, and proactively pursue this life for the sake of your family, using their spiritual and emotional health as your barometer of success. If your family and spouse are doing well, your farm is serving its purpose and will do well in turn. If they are suffering, your farm will suffer, and you are prioritizing the farm for its own sake.

When it comes to moving too fast, don't. That being said, you must move, and you must move now, because if you don't, you likely never will. "Moving" in this context means doing something wherever you find yourself today, not relocating. The term "Back to the Land" deceptively implies that the first step to successful agrarianism is driving your family in a U-Haul to Idaho or [insert preferred agrarian utopia here]. This is a great way to start if you want to destabilize your family with a 90 percent chance of burnout and failure. Unless you grew up on a farm, you have no land to go "back" to, let alone the experience to know what to do with it once you get there. The oft-used term "Flee to the Fields" is even worse. Quaint and radical as it sounds, don't flee anywhere; knee-jerk reactions seldom yield lasting fruit.

A preferable term is "Forward to the Land," the slogan of the 1940s National Catholic Rural Life Conference, but this still places more emphasis on land than on home, lifestyle, and culture. The journey to the land can be a long one, and rushing it will set you up for failure. While access to at least some land at some point is part of the equation, and ownership is a noble long-term goal, remember that you are seeking first a family life that raises saints for God, not primarily the back forty behind the house. And for many families, forty acres is eight to forty times more than what they need.

Pius XII praised "genuine rural culture" over merely "living in the countryside." The Catholic agrarian pursues a way of life before any physical thing or location. Understanding this crucial distinction between location and culture liberates any Catholic family, in any stage of life or type of dwelling, to begin pursuing that culture in their home life before they move anywhere—and sometimes without moving anywhere at all. Once you do obtain land, or access to it by renting, you should be well along the path

by that point, and the journey is far from over. Genuine agrarianism is a Christian way of life, with Heaven as its destination, so
the journey will span our lifetime and continue with our posterity.
We who seek this life in the twenty-first century are reclaiming lost
arts and skills built over centuries of tradition; don't think you
can master them all in a few years. Embrace the lifelong nature
of this journey, celebrate your successes, plan your next steps, get
up when you fall down, and set up your children to take this life
further than you did.

So what is genuine rural culture? Pius XII doesn't leave us
guessing. Rural culture embodies "industriousness, simple and
honest living, respect for authority, especially for parental authority, love of country, and loyalty to traditions ... readiness to aid
one another within the family circle and amongst families, from
home to home." The most distinguishing characteristics, though,
are "You live in continual contact with nature" and "your families are not merely consumer-communities but also and especially
producer-communities." This distinction of the rural household
as a family-based producer-community working with nature is the
sine qua non of genuine Catholic homesteading and consequently
the pathway to success.

The modern family is anything but a producer-community.
With the exception of the kitchen, modern homes are not built
for production, and many kitchens are geared more toward heat-
ing prepared food than transforming raw ingredients into meals.
Society expects homes to be strictly places of shelter for consumers,
where they import food, energy, clothing, services, and electronic
entertainment in exchange for cash earned outside the home.
Society takes for granted that production happens in large fields,
factories, and offices, not in the home. Often zoning laws and
housing communities prohibit anything that resembles production

of vegetables, meat, timber, fiber, construction, or sale of food produced in a home kitchen. The Catholic agrarian rejects this notion of the home and sees it instead through the lens of family productivity. The family that works and prays together stays together.

Families intentionally living this way—frugally making do with what they have, not buying something if they can make it, constantly looking for new ways to increase the productivity of the home and yard they have—will have a successful homestead when they move onto land. They will be successful because to be a homesteader is to be a producer-community that lives and works upon the land, not merely a landowner or countryside dweller. Miss this distinction and you will miss the farm. Lean into it with persistence over time and you will find success. Be willing to live the life before you get the land.

For a young person, couple, or family starting out with homesteading dreams, make an assessment of where you stand on the consumer-producer spectrum. How many meals per week do you cook at home, and how often do you eat out? How many hours do you spend in the home or away? Do you buy new clothes or shop thrift stores for cast offs to modify or mend? Do you make your Christmas gifts or buy them? Do you throw out a sweater when it gets holes in the elbows, or do you learn how to darn? Do you buy bread, yogurt, ketchup, and mayonnaise, or do you make them in your kitchen from raw ingredients? Are you making twice-weekly quick runs to the grocery store, or do you have a well-stocked pantry with dry goods and a chest freezer full of meat purchased from a farmer you know? Are your kids (or you) addicted to processed food? Do you grow and preserve garden produce? Do you send your kids to an expensive school or teach them in your home? Is your yard growing ornamentals or edibles?

Figuring out where you stand as a producer is essential to knowing what the next step is. If your parents never taught you how to cook, learn how to cook. You'll have a lot of food to cook on the homestead. If you never had a vegetable garden growing up, start with some easy vegetables such as zucchini, butternut squash, green beans, cucumbers, and arugula and reduce your grocery bill by a few dollars while you gain crucial skills. If your only childhood animal was a cat, get a small chicken flock (one hen per family member) that you can feed primarily with household food scraps, a practice in frugality and adaption of your production to the capacity of the property you have at hand. Both are essential skills for the homesteader; practice them now.

In your spare time, put your hands on books such as *The Independent Farmstead* by Shawn and Beth Dougherty, *You Can Farm* by Joel Salatin, and *The Market Gardener* by Jean-Martin Fortier, to name only a few. Peruse the catalogs of Acres USA and Chelsea Green. Seek out farmers in your community; look for as many opportunities as possible to spend time with them. Demonstrate willingness to work for free, and jump on volunteer opportunities. Not only will you gain relationships and experience (arguably two of the most useful resources for any homesteader) but your service will pave the way for new opportunities. Be willing to prioritize home production and farm life. Make it a significant portion of your recreation. Once you demonstrate that you are willing to work, are able to learn, and don't cry when you get dirty, you will stand out from the crowd, and you'll be approached with opportunities.

As your budget allows, start accruing some basic tools that will be of use on both a micro scale and on a larger homestead. Common tools such as shovels and rakes can be found at thrift stores and yard sales—don't buy them new. When you do have money for new tools, browse the top tool recommendations from farmer-author Jean-Martin Fortier. Examples include a broad fork, stirrup hoes, a landscape rake, seedling trays, 6 mil. black plastic silage tarps, row cover or insect netting, and wire hoops. With those tools alone, and perhaps a load of purchased (or better yet homemade) compost, you can create a garden in your yard that will grow hundreds of pounds of food. When you move to the land, if you've been practicing at home, you will have a successful garden in the very first year, and it will feel like an old habit.

In addition to relocating too soon, the other critical mistake to avoid is to see your homestead, at least initially, as a commercial enterprise. Just forget trying to make money off any part of it; focus on producing for yourself, and rejoice in the money that is saved. Don't even get too caught up with saving money at first; experience is worth paying for. If you're into homesteading just to cut the bills, you should probably make life easier and visit the local food pantry. Even if you incur cost in the first few years instead of reducing your food budget (a likely scenario), consider it an investment in the skills needed to succeed on a larger scale. Few good things in life come without an initial investment. Be grateful for making the mistakes on a small scale first so you can learn for later.

A corollary to this mindset, which should be obvious, is do not quit your job, especially if you are providing a stable income for your family. God willing, over time your home and homestead will become so productive that you will be able to afford to work less because you need less cash. That's a realistic goal, but it's going to take years to get there. For entrepreneurial folks, you may even turn your farm into a business and derive a living from it, but this is not the way to start. Farm products are not lucrative: they are highly prone to production losses and perishability, and the labor can be intense. In addition, once you divorce the labor from the joy of producing with your family for your own sustenance, the work can quickly become drudgery. Focus on the home, and hang on to your job.

Last but not least, find and encourage others among your peers who are pursuing this life alongside you. Knowing others who are leading productive families of faith will be a great encouragement and support. Ideally they live close by, but don't shy away from cultivating relationships with kindred spirits further abroad. Embody Pius XII's "readiness to aid one another within the family circle and amongst families, from home to home." Share information, experience, tools, labor, and trade; barter farm products, and make bulk purchases together. Get your families together for work, recreation, and prayer.

As you discern your next steps, know that nothing can be lost by bringing your family a little closer together by working on projects, making your home more productive, and thinking twice before purchasing something. Pope St. John XXIII called farming "a vocation, a God-given mission ... undertaken with a view of raising oneself and others to a higher degree of civilization." If you discern in your heart that God has called you and your family along this path, have the patience and trust to know that He will lead you through hard times and show you the way forward, although perhaps only one step at a time. The farm is the native habitat of the family; it will feel like coming home. Keep your eyes fixed on Christ — your feet planted in your home and on the land — and lead your family to sainthood. God is on your side, and you are not alone. Happy homesteading.

Distributism, American Style

ALLAN C. CARLSON

As a philosophy urging the widespread ownership of productive land, family-scale farming, artisanship, strong local economies, and significant household self-sufficiency, distributism found fertile soil in North America. One strain of homegrown ideas and action was best exemplified in the work of Ralph Borsodi. A second strain came as a direct import from G. K. Chesterton's editorial offices, in the person of historian Herbert Agar. Uniting both versions in a distinctive American idiom were the pen and projects of the Jesuit priest John C. Rawe.

Born in 1888 in New York City to immigrant parents from Hungary (Borsodi Beer is still a favorite brand in Budapest!), Ralph Borsodi received no formal education. In contemporary terms, he was homeschooled. His father became active in the Single Tax Movement, inspired by the economic theories of Henry George, which argued that a stiff tax on the speculative value of urban land and buildings was both just and sufficient to fund all the costs of state and local governments. Such a system would leave agricultural land nearly tax free, thus favoring family farms. Among young Borsodi's early mentors was Bolton Hall, author of *A Little Land and a Living*, who made the case for self-sufficient homesteads in the country.

Localism

Following his father's example, Borsodi entered the burgeoning new fields of marketing and advertising. His prominent clients included the National Retail Dry Goods Association and the R. H. Macy department store. In 1911, he married Myrtle May Simpson, an Iowa "farmer's daughter" who had come to the big city seeking work. After their sons were born, the Borsodis looked for an escape from urban grime and crime and moved north to a rundown farmstead on seven acres to the north in Rockland County.

By then, Borsodi was growing increasingly disillusioned with contemporary capitalism. He emphasized the artificial nature of joint-stock corporations, which held privileges—limited liability, perpetual life, and the use of stocks and bonds to raise capital—that laws denied to "natural families." In several books, he showed how large American corporations no longer sought to meet consumer needs. Instead, they worked to "create" needs and swell profits through emotional manipulation in advertising, high pressure marketing, and consumer debt. The consistent goal was to replace "home production for use"—such as gardening, the keeping of chickens, and even maternal breastfeeding—with factory-made products.

Indeed, one of Borsodi's central arguments was that power machinery was a true blessing to human life and liberty, yet it was also a gift blighted by the rise of central factories. As he wrote: "It is the factory, not the machine, which is reducing all men and all commodities to a dead level of uniformity because the factory makes it impossible for individual men and individual communities to be self-sufficient." He continued: "It is the factory, not the machine, which is destroying the skilled craftsman to whom work is a means of self-expression as well as a means of support." Borsodi summarized: "Against the family ... the factory wages a ruthless war of extermination."

The "good news," he reported, was that new, decentralized power sources such as the electrical grid and the internal combustion engine had made possible a liberation from factories. Production could return home, where the family could enjoy most of the efficiencies and gains delivered by the machines. His own research showed that such family-scale production was superior for over two-thirds of the goods and services that the average family consumed.

The Borsodis also "discovered" modern homeschooling. Pulling their boys out of the local school, they found that only two hours a day of coursework was necessary for their children to keep pace with their public-school counterparts. Moreover, the Borsodis learned that true education "was really reciprocal; in the very effort to educate the boys, we educated ourselves."

Building on these insights, Borsodi wrote books, including *Flight from the City* and *Prosperity and Security*, that laid out the arguments for a broad return to self-sufficient homesteads. He also founded The School of Living to train young couples in the forgotten skills of independent living: vegetable gardening, food preservation, poultry and dairy animal care, furniture production, spinning and weaving for family use, and skills for the construction of a house and outbuildings. "The natural family," he affirmed, would be the "normal nucleus" around which to build such a home. Borsodi Homesteads of this sort mushroomed across the land.

And yet there was a problem within Borsodi's otherwise splendid thinking, a moral blackhole. Not only was he an atheist, but militantly so. As he wrote in his bestselling 1929 book *This Ugly Civilization*, "Until we utterly and completely exorcise all religion from our being; until we drop all fears, superstitions, rituals, habits which spring from religion, no true spiritual comfort is possible." Only later would he learn to silence this wholly extraneous side of his advocacy.

Localism

The second, or "imported," strain of distributism came from Herbert Agar. He descended from an old Louisiana family, with modern degrees from a New Jersey prep school and Columbia and Princeton Universities. During a sojourn in England, he turned his attention to analyzing American economic and political woes. As he later wrote, "I had known for years that in some way the America I loved was being strangled, and that it might not survive. But strangled by what?" He found answers in the philosophy expounded by Hilaire Belloc and G. K. Chesterton, which led him to take on an editorial position at the latter's publication, *G. K.'s Weekly.* Here he found men "whose ardor came straight from the French Revolution and whose thought was rooted in the spiritual affirmation of democracy which underlies the Christian faith." Their work "first made it possible for me to recognize the enemy I wanted to fight."

That enemy was finance capitalism, characterized by plutocrats and economic monopolies sustained by corrupt politics. Agar believed that these forces had conspired to destroy free artisans and family farms, consolidating the ownership of land and other productive property into ever fewer hands. This system turned owners into tenants, craftsmen into industrial slaves, and free society into "the servile state." "So far from providing freedom," he wrote, "monopoly capitalism does not even desire it." Indeed, the meaning of "freedom" under the rule of the plutocrats had been inverted: "In terms of labor ... a workman had better be 'free' from a home, because if he had a home he would not be sufficiently mobile." Moreover, he had better be "free" from all family bonds; "above all, he had better be free from children."

In his Pulitzer Prize–winning history of the American Presidency, *The People's Choice,* Agar traced the corruptions of "money-based democracy" through the nation's past, from Washington to

Harding. "The story of America is a tale of repeated revolts" against the capitalists, he said. These had never triumphed, because "the temptation to betray" true liberty had always been "as compelling as the urge to uphold it." Democracy "normally culminates in dictatorship; the money-anarchy makes way for the tyrant-state." Still, "so long as the revolts occur—often and with intensity—we can continue hoping that some day we may become a free land and a true democracy."

In the distributist spirit, Agar condemned "world cities" such as London, Chicago, and New York for their clear signs of decadence. Moral relativity or the equal truth of all gods was another sign here. Agar referred to a prominent New York writer who had praised the Aztec leader Montezuma, adding in still very relevant words: "It is right that he should approve of Montezuma's relativism: world-city is talking to world-city, and they speak the same language. Montezuma was a 'civilized' man. He knew that all truths are relative."

Instead of fretting over "civilization," Agar—in the spirit of Chesterton—urged that first attention go to local cultures. As he wrote in arguably his best book, *Land of the Free,* "The country town is still rooted in the land about it. The relation between town and countryside is still organic," and healthy. Public policy should aim at the support of agrarian farmers, small town merchants, and decentralized factories.

Agar was not, apparently, a believing Christian of any sort. All the same, he praised Roman Catholicism as a force for good. Where Protestant thought tended to favor the concentration of ownership in a few hands and easy credit for the rich, the Catholic Church "traditionally favored small property," hard money, and "widely distributed ownership." Catholic social thought also affirmed agrarianism as "the system in which the farmer first makes himself, his family, and his beasts, as self-supporting as possible," selling only those surpluses that remained.

Herbert Agar was also skilled at building coalitions. In June 1936, he took the lead in organizing a meeting of agrarian and distributist leaders in Nashville, Tennessee. Ralph Borsodi was there, along with leading members of the Southern Agrarians loosely tied to Vanderbilt University. The group adopted a statement of economic and political principles that featured key distributist themes. It opposed the denial of economic freedom found under communism, fascism, *and* finance capitalism. It demanded an end to "the sacrifice of agriculture for the development of manufacture" while giving recognition "to the primacy of agriculture in establishing a secure and desirable culture." Governments should actively help those "families desiring to work land and to live on it" gain ownership of tracts "sufficient to sustain them in security and comfort." Another product of this gathering was a decision to launch a monthly distributist magazine. Named *Free America*, it first appeared the following January. Agar and Borsodi were two of the founding editors, joined by philanthropist (and later Catholic convert) Chauncey Stillman.

Also in attendance at the Nashville session was the Jesuit scholar John C. Rawe. Born and raised on a central Illinois farm, he attended St. Louis University, earning degrees in Law. He also resolved to enter the Society of Jesus. In the early 1930s, he studied theology at St. Mary's College and Seminary in Kansas. He joined there a "zealous seminar of rural life advocates," turning him into the most vigorous American Catholic intellectual voice of the era for distributist and agrarian principles. His early essays picked up on legal and constitutional themes raised by Borsodi. Rawe blasted U.S. federal court decisions that had transformed commercial corporations into "artificial persons" bearing "rights" that the Founders had intended for real humans alone. On this basis, Big Business had since battered family-scale farms, stores, and manufacturing shops, building monopolies in their place and concentrating property ownership in ever fewer hands.

Public policy must now intervene to rebuild a truly democratic and humane order. As Rawe explained regarding agriculture, "rich acres and productive plants are safe only in the hands of a small owner, . . . a family man, who can respect and cooperate with the laws of nature, make provision for crop rotation, prevent erosion, and give paternal care to the plants and animals that feed and shelter him and his dear ones." Toward this end, Rawe also emphasized that families must reinvigorate as productive units. Under the joint regime of Big Government and Big Business, both the marriage and birth rates had withered. Rawe's response: "We must have a rising birth rate. We must have a new vitality in Christian home life and home culture." The "only way" to do this, he said, was to restore the productive home, "where the child could soon become an economic asset instead of remaining an economic liability." Toward this end, Rawe urged that future home construction include "school and work rooms" and be located on small acreages.

Over a ten-year span that ended with his early death in 1946, Rawe further developed such ideas in an important series of essays and books. In 1939, for example, he was the "ghost" author of *A Manifesto on Rural Life*, a rich and lively document issued by the Bishops of Fargo and Bismarck in North Dakota. The next year he co-authored the "Summa" of Catholic Agrarianism, *Rural Roads to Security: America's Third Struggle for Freedom*. Where co-author Fr. Luigi Ligutti focused on pastoral and educational matters, Rawe wrote the more ideologically charged chapters. He openly called here for a "Green Revolution," a new American campaign for liberty to be founded on "family unit operation and . . . family-basis ownership of land based on religious principles."

Indeed, through his forceful reconciliation of Catholicism with agrarianism, John Rawe did resolve the most serious problems afflicting American distributism in the mid-twentieth century. Most directly, he showed how the arguments employed by the atheist Ralph Borsodi and the agnostic Herbert Agar actually gained power and clarity when reframed in an openly Christian manner. Moreover, where many other Catholic writers of the era looked back wistfully to the European Middle Ages as their ideal, Fr. Rawe was an unabashed American. The social and political order that he sought to restore was that of Jefferson (on his better days), not that of Thomas Aquinas.

Finally, John C. Rawe offered up an environmental ethic that displayed a welcome form of enchantment without descending into Druidism. Writers Christopher Hamlin and John McGreevy show that where others saw beauty and value in wild and scenic places, Rawe focused on "organic processes and temporal cycles." For him, nature was not sacred; however, "work in nature *was* sacramental," centered on "sky and soil, watching small parts of nature change through the seasons."

In these ways, Fr. Rawe's legacy may lie in a contemporary rediscovery of his distributist writings by young American Roman Catholics searching for an agrarian environmental ethic fully compatible with their faith.

A Common Enterprise

CHRISTOPHER CHECK

Jacqueline and I have been breeding and showing Cavalier King Charles Spaniels—famed companions of the Stuart kings—since 2007. I should clarify: Jackie does the heavy lifting. She researches the genetics of sires and dams and their ancestors so that our puppies meet the standards of the breed. She manages breeding and whelping. She oversees vetting and vaccinating. She exhibits our Cavaliers in the show ring (we have never used a hired handler!). What is my role? I am the unpaid kennel help. Use your imagination.

Our kennel is named Top Meadow Cavaliers after G. K. Chesterton's Beaconsfield estate. Chesterton, alas, was not a spaniel man. He owned an Aberdeen Terrier named Quoodle, immortalized in a poem celebrating the things dogs appreciate but men, because of our fallen nature, do not: the "wind of winter forests" and "the breath of brides adorning" and the true smell of roses.

In his essay, "On Keeping a Dog," Chesterton goes further and suggests that dogs understand us more clearly than we do: "But my dog knows I am a man, and you will not find the meaning of that word written in any book as clearly as it is written in his soul." Perhaps the next public official asked to say what a man is should ask a dog, but Chesterton, who knows what both are, wastes no time puzzling over the singular relationship between men and dogs. So much of it—like all of God's gifts—is confined to the realm of mystery. He is content to say:

> Somehow this creature has completed my manhood; somehow, I cannot explain why, a man ought to have a dog. A man ought to have six legs; those other four legs are part of him. Our alliance is older than any of the passing and priggish explanations that are offered of either of us; before evolution was, we were.

Needless to say, lines like those have never been penned about a goldfish or a ferret, much less about that doubtful Egyptian contribution to the world of pets, the housecat. Frank Sheed felt pretty certain that the Holy Family did not own a cat, and if a painting that hangs in the Prado by Bartolomé Esteban Murillo can be taken as proof positive (and why not?), the Holy Family did own a dog, and a spaniel at that. It is a sentimental scene showing Our Lady and St. Joseph looking on with fondness as the Child Jesus seems to tease the family dog with a bird he holds in his hand. Mary spins, and behind Joseph rest the plane, square, and saw of a carpenter. Spindle and workbench are in the background, but for the soul who takes a moment to contemplate the painting, a deep reality of family life comes into focus. Undergirding domestic joy is something not common in modern households: common enterprise.

Not long ago, Jackie and I were asked by a young lady and her fiancé for counsel. So we marshalled friends we thought represented the institution well and hosted a dinner. Over some vermicelli with pesto and plenty of Chianti, we shared secrets of success. Jackie's and my contribution? The benefits of a common family enterprise, in our case, Top Meadow Cavaliers.

Our four sons are largely launched, but when they were young, they were there to help with whelping, they took their shifts with new pups to be sure they were feeding and gaining weight, and they wrestled crates in and out of the van for trips to the vet and the show ring. Puppy buyers who came to the house and met our sons learned that our Cavaliers were bred and raised in a lively and loving home.

Our little kennel is hardly the kind of common enterprise that was at the center of the home in Nazareth. St. Joseph actually supported his family with the family business. We are happy when puppy sales cover showing, breeding, veterinary expenses, and, in good years, the occasional tuition payment. Nonetheless, whether we should call Top Meadow a family business or a family hobby, the kennel is a common family activity, a kind of way of living the fullness of family life a world in which most homes are little more than mortgages on a sphere of consumption.

The fullness of family life? Long before the pills and promiscuity of the sexual revolution broke apart so many marriages, the industrial revolution broke the family bonds formed by common enterprise. Once upon a time, all households were centers of production—farms, workshops, forges, shops—marked by family ownership of the means of production. What happened? First men and then women were taken, as my friend Allan Carlson puts it in the title of his superb book, *From Cottage to Work Station*. Two centuries later, it is not only the kind of productive work that generates revenue that has been taken from the home but even more fundamental functions once done in common. Meal preparation is an obvious example, but another is entertainment. Guitars, fiddles, and storytelling are given over entirely to earbuds and screens, each family member with his own device. Could we be more atomized?

The ideal antidote is a family business staffed by parents and children, but if this distributist ideal is out of reach for most of us, strengthening of family bonds through common work is not.

Of foremost importance is the strengthening of the marital bond, and very few children today have come of age with the example of husband-and-wife laboring alongside each other. We think of husbands and wives more as companions or friends, ideally, lifelong. Sure, they are united in the rearing of children, but contraception, in enabling married couples to turn away from or at least discount this primary end of marriage, has reinforced the idea of a "companionate" marriage. *Humanae Vitae* dissenter Michael Novak argued in 1969 that contraception would deepen marital love, through—as he irreverently riffed off Pope St. Pius X—"frequent, even daily, communion."

We now know Novak was wrong (so does he), that contraception divides couples, but along with be fruitful and multiply, God commanded Adam and Eve to subdue the earth. Might theologians give more attention to common enterprise as an essential element of a complete marriage, particularly in an age when non-marriage has replaced marriage as the social norm? For at least a decade now, most households in America are not married-couple households. While divorce remains a culprit, what is striking is the growing number of young people who never marry in the first place. Marriage rates are lower than ever in the history of the West. Catholics are not immune. To blame is a widespread impression of marriage that is distorted or, at least, incomplete.

If more children, however, had the daily example of a man and his wife working out their differences, and growing closer as a result, in fulfilling their responsibilities to the family business, they would be more likely to understand through this very practical manifestation that marriage in the fullness of its expression involves effort and self-denial, that it requires husband and wife letting go of their own inclinations in favor of a united adventure.

Chesterton is famous for praising the family as "an uncongenial institution," one in which its members are smoothed by rubbing against one another. Pursuit of a common goal provides the context for this effect that the spouses first, and then all the family members, work on each other. The more challenging the effort the better. Yes, it's delightful to be in the back yard grilling, singing songs, and tossing horseshoes on a Sunday afternoon, and these occasions bind us, but not nearly as much as working our way through the daily successes and failures of a common enterprise. A child who sees a marriage strengthened by common labor knows so much more about spousal love than the child who merely witnesses Mom and Dad heading off each Thursday for date night.

Nothing wrong with date night, I feel compelled to say. If you are married and haven't had one in a while, go out to dinner. At dinner, decide to unite in a common enterprise.

Your first litter won't be far behind.

Localism: In Theory and Practice

David W. Cooney

The problem of discussing localism is that it can mean different things to different people. Many people only consider certain aspects of the local community when advocating what they call localism, but what would a more complete localist view of the economy entail? I propose that a truly localist economy is one in which the members and businesses of the local community consider that community to be their primary sphere of economic activity – and where the businesses of that community are not only local in terms of physical location but are independently and locally owned and controlled so they can adjust to serve the needs and wants of that local community.

This does not mean that those who advocate localism are isolationists. A localist community would still trade with other communities far and wide, but it would also make sure that, as much as possible, its economy did not become dependent on that activity. The community would work to structure itself so that as many of its basic needs as possible are produced by its own members, and it would support that production by consistently going to those producers for the majority, if not all, of their basic needs. Trade with other communities would generally be seen as a means of acquiring non-essentials and experiencing the unique things other communities have to offer.

Contrast this explanation of localism to what many people might be thinking. Some people don't go much further than supporting local farmers at the local farmer's market and some locally owned shops, but when it comes to other types of products, they do not think it's that important that the actual producer of them should be local. Others who say they are strong advocates of local businesses include businesses that are contractually controlled by non-local corporations through franchise agreements. They might even include large warehouse stores that happen to exist in the local community even though they are owned and run by large corporations far away from their local community.

However, for those who are trying to envision a truly localist society, the local community is the heart that keeps the flow of economic activity moving in order to keep the local community alive. In other words, the movement of money within and throughout the local community's economy is like the flow of blood through the human body. If too much of it is directed out of the community, it will get sick and eventually die. This is a truly different mindset from our current economic environment where local communities are kept alive by a sort of dialysis known as the supply chain of national and international distribution systems.

So what exactly does it mean to really have a local economy? It means believing that without a good, strong, local economy to support it, the local community is weak and dependent no matter how much neat stuff the average person may own or how nice the cars in the driveways are. It means supporting the local producer and provider as much as possible. If you are your neighbors' customer, and they are yours, then you mutually support each other, and money will flow throughout the local economy. The best way to support the local economy is to be the customer of local, independently owned businesses to the greatest extent you can. It also means we have to have a clear idea of what really constitutes a "local" and "independently owned" business.

A truly local business is not simply one that exists within a local community. In the sense I am using here, "local business" means the business is integrated into the whole local economy and supports it as much as it practically can; the term does not just reference a physical location. To really be a local business, the local economy needs to be an integral aspect of its business operation. The local community is its primary customer base, and, as much as possible, it is also a customer to other local businesses within the community. A business in a community that exclusively, or even mostly, has a customer base of those who live outside the community is not local business because it doesn't serve the local community, and a business that does not take the opportunity to be a customer to other local businesses is not a local business in this sense because it doesn't support the local economy. An exception to this idea might be something like an inn for tourists, but this is the general rule.

Just as "local" encompasses more than physical location, the concept of "independently owned" encompasses more than mere legal ownership. Ownership is not truly independent unless the owner is free to adapt the business to meet local needs and wants without having to go through outside approval first. This excludes a business that is bound, by its incorporation or by some contract, to let some non-local board of directors dictate how it does business. Most franchise businesses, therefore, would not qualify as being an "independently owned" business in this sense. Uniformity is required by the typical franchise business. Depending on the franchise agreement, the owner of a franchise might not be free to choose the look of his business, the clothing of his employees, the type of furnishings, what suppliers he uses, how much his employees are paid, what benefits are offered to the employees, what products he offers, or how they are prepared and delivered to the customer. Many franchises require that the owners purchase from their corporate headquarters not only the products they sell but also the furnishings of the franchise establishment, which means they are restricted from being customers to other local businesses. Likewise, a local outlet of a large corporation headquartered and managed outside of the local community also does not qualify as a local, independently owned business. It is not enough merely to provide jobs within the community; the primary flow of its economic activity must be within that community. If the profits are siphoned off to corporate offices somewhere else rather than to those who live, work, and do business in the community, it really isn't a local business in the sense we are advocating.

The type of self-sufficiency we advocate for localism is based on the idea that a local community must be able to produce as much of its basic needs as possible, such as construction, textiles, metal crafts, and many other things needed to produce housing, clothing, and other useful items. When considering basic needs, however, we must not forget one of the most basic of all: food. Localists don't necessarily say we need to return to an agrarian society, but economic independence for communities necessarily includes agricultural independence to the greatest extent possible. Therefore, local communities, including large cities, would need to consider how to incorporate a robust agricultural sector as local as possible to support that independence. This agricultural sector, like the rest of the localist economy, would be comprised of a large number of independent producers rather than large farms that have to operate through tightly controlled distribution centers that ship products all across the country. Of course, localism also encourages any families that want to be even partially self-sufficient by growing food for themselves.

There are two distinct advantages to having widespread owner-ship of local agriculture. The first advantage is that it brings food production into the community, making the community more independent because it is more self-sufficient. The local commu-nity will have more control over what foods are available to them because the local farmers will need to meet the needs of its primary customer—the local community. The local community will also be more assured that their food will be good quality, since when food production is local to the community, the production process will be more visible to the customers, and if local farmers need to maintain good relationships with their local communities, they will work to meet their community's high standards of quality. The other advantage is that whenever a problem with food production occurs, the impact is minimized, and other local food production, both local to the community and from nearby communities, can offset a shortage in most cases. This means there would be less reliance on government programs for such things.

Now those of us who advocate for a truly localist view realize that there are some practical limitations to this ideal. We acknowledge that there are some industries that would be completely impracti-cal to have in every community, at least with current technology. Therefore, there are some businesses that will need to be more regional than local. Take cars and similar vehicles, for example. It is impractical to suggest that every local community should have its own auto makers. However, there is no economic law that says the United States should only have the "Big Three" automobile manufacturers. We used to have many more manufacturers spread throughout the country. Capitalism's tendency to consolidate wealth into the hands of fewer and fewer people is the only reason we don't have a wide variety of independent automobile manufacturers today. The same could be said for many other industries. From the localist perspective, these types of industries would also better serve their regional communities if they were independently owned worker cooperatives.

At this point, I feel the need to make it clear that we are not advocating the seizure of existing corporations by governments to redistribute their ownership. What I'm speaking of here is a change of mood, a new philosophical outlook at the consumer level. If each of us actively chose to support businesses that fit the truly localist economic model as much as we could, the transition to a fully localist economic model would take place naturally, without significant economic disruption, and without the need for government redistribution.

There are many organizations dedicated to promoting the viability of worker-owned cooperatives for large businesses, and there are many examples that prove that the ideas of the localist movement are both achievable and practical. Many localists point to Mondragón as one example of how well this model can work. Mondragón started as a technical college in Spain, founded by Fr. José María Arizmendiarrieta in 1943. Its first cooperative was established with five workers making paraffin heaters in 1955. Today, Mondragón is a cooperative federation comprising more than 250 companies and 74,000 workers operating in the finance, industrial, retail, and knowledge sectors. They have 15 technology centers and 1,676 researchers, and they have filed 479 patents.

The worker-owners of Mondragón achieved such success by pooling their resources. They did not rely on government support. Each company agrees to set its own wage ratio within an agreed upon range of 3:1 to 9:1. The average is 5:1, meaning that the highest paid person in a given company typically makes no more than five times what the lowest paid person in the same company does. The result is that the workers doing non-management jobs at Mondragón typically make 13 percent more than similar local jobs outside of its structure. Most workers make well above the minimum wage, since they are employed in jobs requiring high levels of skill and technical training. Mondragón's managers do earn less than those outside of its structure, but this is because they agree that Mondragón's model is better than the typical corporate model.

We have to remember that Mondragón operates in a capitalist economy, and it has grown to a size and scale of operation beyond what can be considered truly local. Nevertheless, Mondragón proves beyond any reasonable doubt that the cooperative model works. Advocates of both localism and the cooperative movements therefore propose this model for large-scale operations, particularly those that make sense at a more regional level.

What is preventing local communities from achieving truly local economies? The sad truth is that the members of the local communities themselves are. This is not necessarily their fault. They've been raised in a predominantly capitalist society. They've been educated in schools run by a government that is beholden to capitalist economic power. Other than exposure to some collectivist views in school or at home, what else do they know?

While it is true that capitalism is not opposed to local businesses or local economy, its structure and practices tend heavily toward the consolidation of production and wealth, which results in weakening local economies by making them dependent on centralized production. By and large, the average person has been trained all his life to be an employee. Those who truly accept this training might be allowed to manage their fellow employees in large companies owned by corporations of shareholders. They accept, by training and habit, their role in what can be called the "socio-capitalistic feudalism" under which we live. The average member of the local community has never been given the tools to understand adequately the full implications of the points we are trying to make.

So the changes needed to transition to a truly localist economy will take time to occur. We are asking people to take on a whole new attitude about economics, government, and their role in society. We are asking them to abandon the "employee" mindset and to take risks—even if it is just the risk of continuing to support the small local shop as long as it manages to last.

Convincing people, however, requires more than simplistic platitudes against the rich and railing against capitalism. Until they understand that they really can achieve ownership, and why they should consider it better that there should be many owners rather than few, people won't consider themselves as potentially anything other than employees. Until they understand how the local businesses and employees support each other by being each other's customers, they won't understand how circulation of economic activity among locally owned businesses within a local community strengthens the local economy in ways that chain stores and franchises do not, and they won't see the true importance of the local economy.

Until they understand how keeping the majority of their economic activity local stabilizes that economy and makes their own shop or job more secure, they won't fully understand how the loss of a local business to a big chain is bad for the local economy and contributes to the potential loss of their own business or job in that community. Until they see how having a thriving local community with lots of locally owned businesses creates more opportunities for trade with other communities with their own local economies, they won't understand how their local economy impacts other local economies and the jobs within those communities. Until they understand how having a strong local economy with lots of locally owned businesses is essential to both their negotiating power as employees and their prospects for becoming a business owner, they won't understand how having the presence of a big chain store that offers things at prices below market value is corrosive to their own opportunities. Until they see how the interaction of many businesses supporting each other and being an interactive part of the local community affects things like cost and supply, they won't question why the big chain stores can offer goods at below-market prices—prices that don't adequately support the people producing the goods and providing the services. Until they question why big business can offer goods and services at below-market prices, they won't really think much about the government subsidies or atrocious working conditions that combine with a massive government-subsidized distribution system to make those prices possible.

Until they see all of this, they won't understand that they are actually being cheated by the lower prices of large, multi-national corporations, because those low prices come with a very high, hidden cost: independence, economic security, and ultimately, freedom.

Loving Place Practically

CHARLES A. COULOMBE

If the rioting and burning of the summer of 2020 taught us nothing else, it is that local government—which we tend to ignore at the media's bidding—is still very important; for too long, too many of us have ignored it. Certainly, many who live in the countless bedroom communities surrounding every major American city are blissfully ignorant of whomever their mayors and city councilmen may be. This elective ignorance in turn leads to a sort of "dictatorship of the involved," wherein the small minority actually interested in civic affairs dominate perforce, in lieu of the uninterested majority. My own Los Angeles suburb, for example, has been taken over by a benign coalition of historic home preservationists and downtown merchants: in return for their complete control, they have given us wonderful police protection, excellent library and other services, and a full civic calendar, filled with fun events for the whole family. But many similar towns have seen instead a reign of greedy grifters lining their pockets thanks to blissful ignorance.

But these concerns are on a purely utilitarian level. Beyond them is the question of patriotism and of love of one's fellow man—indeed, of humanity in general. Before we start trick-or-treating for UNICEF or waving the flag to show either of these on our own parts, we must remember that all of these sorts of love begin with the lowest possible unit: the family. Our family in so many ways determines who we are and how we see ourselves. So we should endeavor to be proud of its accomplishments and add to them by our own efforts. This is why genealogy can be so important—not for matters of snob appeal but to give us more knowledge of who we are and to inspire ourselves and (more importantly) our young folk to add to or create luster for our name. At the same time, if our bloodline entitles us to join any hereditary societies, we should do so, especially if they have local branches engaged in things worth doing.

Now let's go further: into the neighborhood. We may have lived there all our lives, just moved in, or anywhere between. It may be a poor or wealthy urban ward, a suburban bedroom community, or a rural village. Whatever the case, it has a history and heritage all its own (about which we probably don't know much). As with our family in space and time, we cannot begin to properly love it until we know it. The best place to begin is our parish.

Our church is not just where we go to receive the sacraments, vital as those are. It is a community with a history—and one of the building blocks of our locale. It is not just that we should become active in it and whichever of its organizations fit us, we should learn as much as we can about it: its founding priest and his successors, the pioneer families, and the history of the building and its fittings. We should pray for its dead donors, so often commemorated on window and pew. We should learn its boundaries. Moreover, we should encourage our pastor and help out as we can with existing festivals and outdoor processions. The ultimate witness of our Faith is a procession with the Blessed Sacrament on Rogation Days, Corpus Christi, and the feast of Christ the King. Our parish is an important part of the heritage of our community at large.

But just what is that heritage? It is actually a far wider category than we often think. The website of the small, French town of Sèvres-Anxaumont has a wonderful definition of heritage in general:

> When we talk about heritage, we immediately think of the built heritage, that is to say of the churches, the castles, the beautiful manors of yesteryear. We also generally include what is called the "small heritage," namely crosses, funerary monuments, wash houses or vine huts if there are any.
>
> But many other areas are heritage. This is first of all the case with the geographical setting and in particular the relief, but also the watercourses and the climate, because these elements largely condition the landscapes—which are also modified by human intervention.
>
> The local flora is also part of our heritage. These are both spontaneous flora and plants traditionally cultivated in a particular place. Thus the small local orchids deserve our attention, just as much as the large chestnut trees in process of decline. The local fauna is also part of the heritage, whether it is wild fauna, ranging from large game to the smallest insects of the lawn or domestic animals and their local breeds adapted to the soil.
>
> The people who came before us should also hold our attention. They can be personalities who have influenced local or national life. It is just as much about the generations of modest people who have left their mark on the territory. Their way of life, their professional activities, their mentality have left lasting traces. This is why we have an interest in looking at local history, in connection with national history. So let's get to know better all that remains of agricultural, craft and industrial activity, as well as the

dialect, often revealing ways of thinking, legends and popular songs, cooking recipes.

By becoming aware of all these elements, we will better understand where we come from and who we are, we will be able to better respect and protect this heritage and, having added our own contribution, we will be able to pass it on to future generations more easily.

I would add that this wonderful patrimony to which we are heirs and of which we are perforce custodians ought to be seen not merely as the relics of bygone glory but as the building blocks of a better future—in our urban ward or rural village; in our county; in our province, state, or region; in our country; in the Christian West, from San Francisco to Vladivostok (hence my interest in the Council of Europe's Cultural Routes scheme); and indeed, in the world as a whole (which is why I find the World, Intangible, Forest, and Agricultural Heritage Programs of UNESCO and FAO among the few U.N. efforts worth investigating). Whether it be folklore and dance, the local waterfall, literary societies, or the efforts of noble or hereditary societies to conserve their traditions, these relics of our heritage deserve whatever support we can give them—and it is so horrible when "wokery" sticks its snout into these things.

While not as important as our religious efforts, these concerns certainly complement them and are in their way more important than any mere political party effort. I urge you as strongly as I can to support as you are able in time and/or money these treasures in your own sphere that take your fancy. Do some exploring, either online or in reality. Wikipedia can reveal to you sites in your county on the National Register of Historic Places, and most communities have historic societies, land trusts, parks, museums, and the like worth discovering. Treat your home as though you were a tourist, and contact the local tourism and visitor's bureau for recreational ideas. Get to know your neighborhood library and join its "friends of" group. Participate in local festivities, parades, and observances to the best of your ability. Are there local theater or musical events you can attend or support? You enjoy sports? Fine! Forget about watching the too-often "woke" pros on TV; get out and support your local high school and amateur teams.

But love of place means more than just valuing and supporting the local heritage; the local economy deserves support as well. Many places have "shop-local Saturdays" and the like, on which participants make a point of avoiding the chains and only patronizing local businesses; but see to what degree you can do this sort of shopping more and more on a regular basis—despite the increased expense. Explore the local co-ops and farmer's markets.

Most activities are sponsored by volunteer groups; many of these groups are found in nearly every community: the Knights of Columbus, VFW, American Legion, Kiwanis, Rotary, Elks, and the like. If you can find the time, participating in these groups and in their many activities can be personally very rewarding in terms of the experiences you'll have and friendships you'll make. But beyond this personal scope, you'll also help to make the place you live in a better one.

That having been said, especially if you are a newcomer, and depending upon where you are, you shall doubtless find already ensconced a spider's web of entrenched interests, and you may very quickly see ways in which things can be improved. It is highly unwise to share the latter prematurely. To avoid antagonizing the powers that be, make it clear that you have not come to empire-build but to help achieve the common goal, which should be more important to you than holding office or achieving recognition—and be sure to choose only those activities whose goal really *does* excite you. In time, as you demonstrate to the others your sincerity and your willingness to sacrifice time and energy on the common effort, they will very likely welcome any ideas or suggestions.

This understanding may carry over to local politics. If you do choose to enter this field, you must do so out of real love of the place and out of a real desire to improve and enhance it. Local government often features a host of positions that are poorly paid or entirely volunteer. In my town, most elected officials generally run unopposed. Outside of big cities with their party machines, the group that runs a town is generally fairly insular. If you think they are doing a good job, offer to help where needed. If not, make sure your objections are well-founded—and that you have actively pursued the volunteerism I suggested—and you will have a ready-made electoral base.

For the Catholic, however, his patriotism for his community cannot be limited to the heritage, cultural, economic, and political aspects of his dwelling place—he must also think of the spiritual: that means evangelism. Now you cannot evangelize what you do not love, and you cannot love what you do not know—so in a real sense, everything we have spoken of so far was in preparation for your evangelizing work. You love your town, and a great many of your fellow townsmen know and like you. If you do receive any acknowledgment, make it known that living your Faith was the major factor in what you did. Let your Catholic life be as open as possible. Always invite non-Catholic friends to such things as Baptisms, Confirmations, First Communions, and weddings, and make sure to entertain them at accompanying festivities. They shall want to know what it's all about. Make sure that any historical contributions by Catholics in your neighborhood are as well-known as possible. Assist your pastor and parish to whatever degree you are allowed to make the sorts of observances earlier noted and the Liturgy in general as impressive as possible. Invite folks to these liturgical celebrations as well—especially those in honor of the local patron saints.

To be sure, this is an ambitious program for anyone, and we are all limited by time, money, and interests. But for too long our attention has been directed to the world, national, and sometimes state levels, where we count for very little as individuals. But on the local level—even if our town does not have town meetings in the New England style—not only can we count, but often enough, simply participating shall give us an influence all out of proportion. Moreover, if we can help make our parish, city ward, suburb, or village a better, happier, more unified place, we and ours may well survive in a better manner the coming challenges facing our country, state, nation, continent, and planet. "Think globally, act locally" may itself be an annoying New Age mantra, but it describes what Catholics have been doing since Jesus sent us out of the Holy Land.

Downstream from Real Life

Jason Craig

There's a debate among social commentators about the interaction of politics and culture: are politics "downstream from culture," or is culture downstream of politics? I find the debate worth having, though I feel no compelling reason to try to settle it. I must answer less esoteric problems, like whether to try to plant a bigger garden to offset inflated food prices or to encourage my children to avoid the scams that many colleges have become. My problems are bigger because I'm a father, and whatever the societal disorder, dad is usually downstream of it all. From tax policies to new gadgets vying for attention (and money), a father is often a man that must deal with it in some way. The tension between globalism and localism is no different. In fact, the father might just be at the center of it.

There's a polite pretending that some of us feel compelled to engage in, wherein we speak as if fathers are not "in charge" of households the way they were when the word "patriarchy" was good and not a slur. Yet those regularly engaged with family life know that every home is shaped in some way by the father. Fathers lead and direct their homes for good or ill, causing sickness or health. Whether the home has a weak, strong, or even abusive father, he is leading and imprinting his personality on that household's members. A father's role is so unavoidably impactful to the formation of a family that even his *absence* matters, fatherlessness being a leading cause of all sorts of societal disorders and problems. Even if decapitated, the father is still the head of the home.

I suppose it must be said—though I wish it didn't—that the headship of a father is no exercise of raw power and control, at least from a Christian perspective. Friedrich Engels, the father of Marxist philosophy, famously categorized the father as a tyrannical power maintained by economic dominance, likening wife and children to the proletariat masses controlled by their subjugation to the bourgeoisie. But Engels had the luxury of being able to hypothesize a world without *paterfamilias* because the family in his time was a cultural force. But we, downstream of the culture and politics Marxism has so affected, know better at this point. From religious practice to economic mobility to violence, there are few measures of health that we can't relate back to the value and necessity of a good father.

Therefore, any hope for a more localized social and economic culture requires the presence and dedication of fathers. That's because what Engels had right was that the authority and influence of a father is fundamentally linked to the economic interaction of home and society. He is often like a bridge between the two worlds, being a point of integration or division. Globalized economics and crushing corporatism bypass the normative and natural relations that form and nurture the identities of man. Therefore, crushing the father's local and economic bonds in a community and home is the disruption of the very nature and needs of the family. Because the father is so central in the bridging between society and household—as a fact of his vocation to protect and provide—robust assistance and consideration of his role is not optional. Consolidating powers don't grow from nothing. They rise from consolidating and abrogating authority and resources from local communities. Gigantism and localism are at odds because they're in competition for the same turf. When a father stands at the threshold of home and community, however, he is protector as much as provider. By recovering the sanity of localism, a father strengthens his relationships in the home, which cultivates stable and authentic community, and sets up a bullwork against the abuses from without.

I. Localism and Relationships in the Home

In a traditional and local economy, the work of a father is outside the home, but still nearby. His work serves as a means of connection and cohesion that we have a hard time imagining today. It also integrates all members, freeing us from the strange ideal—that some love and some hate—of the father leaving all day and the wife staying home for housework. Home-based and local work was simply more than the simplistic division between paying for the house and keeping it clean. The work differed by the obvious differences of the sexes and their physical capabilities, but in essence, it was a shared responsibility that required careful communication and cooperation. Without such shared and approximate work, familial relationships can become more strained, as we have a hard time knowing exactly what the family is *for*.

We tend to think of the institution of the family as essentially relational, there to fulfill psychological and emotional needs. It is no secret that fathers are not the best captains for that sort of ship. Or, put differently, if the family is primarily a form of emotional support and formation, and the father is its head, then we should suspect that unless a man has a unique relational ability (which some have, but few), then the family will suffer. Robert

Nisbet helps us see why the modern conception ironically makes the relational bonds more difficult. In former times, says Nisbet, "the family was the actual agency of economic production, distribution, and consumption." The father did not have to "balance" family and work life because they were part of the same *institution*. Today, by contrast, the family "has progressed from institution to companionship," says Nisbet, by losing the bonds created when the home has tangible *function* for life beyond sleeping, eating, and "hanging out." It is actually hard for us to think of a family as *dysfunctional* when it is united in shared work—that word seems uniquely reserved to how we relate today. This isn't to say that family businesses don't cause arguments, but that they give utility and function to a family.

Nisbet goes on to claim there is little hope that attentiveness to feelings and support devoid of practical connection will be enough to keep the family institution strong: "[To] suppose that at present the family ... can perpetually vitalize itself through some indwelling affectional tie, in the absence of concrete, perceived functions, is like supposing that the comradely tied of mutual aid [in] a military unit will long outlast a condition in which war is plainly and irrevocably banished." As sociologists have been observing since the industrial revolution, the lack of shared, practical, and functional orientation has depleted the family's bondedness and, therefore, rootedness to place and each other.

II. Overworking?

Today, we know fathers are pulled from their homes to work, often to the point of being charged with workaholism. Of the father it is said he forgets his family's needs because "all he cares about is work." It is true that a man's work orients outwardly to the point he can snap the bonds to his family if he's not careful. He goes hunting for the hunt and forgets he's really out there to feed his family. Yet I think a defense must be made here, and it too is related to the difference between the integrated work of localism and the balancing act of many modern jobs.

The nature of visible work, and the local connection of it, strengthens and proves the bond of work and home. The ever-lovable "Pa" from Laura Ingalls Wilder's *Little House* series is endlessly engaged in some matter of work. He is plowing, planting, building, digging, harvesting, hunting, tanning, and so on. In Wilder's *Farmer Boy*, Almanzo, the central character of the book, has a father that even works when he is at rest with his family, rubbing glass on an ax handle as they sit by the fire at night after dinner (this smooths and preserves a new handle).

Yet the care and character of these fathers are manifest and enviable. Their children are near the work, see the work, and respect the work—and in the work, they see, taste, and believe the dedication of their father to his work is really a dedication to them. But they're not merely spectators, but participants—and this mentoring arrangement provides further opportunities for more organically strengthened relationships.

III. It Makes a Village

The relational benefits of economic integration and localism doesn't stop in the home. Today, many of us know that we have to engage in that seemingly unnatural act of the will called "intentional community." We must be intentional because our daily lives, dominated by the practical cares of work, pull us constantly away from our community. Community, then, becomes an act of will—its intentionality. But just as the family loses its vitality when it becomes solely about companionship but is devoid of institutional (cultural and political) strength, so too a community can be drained of something essential when it lacks functional connections. Localism, by contrast, cultivates community.

(I would add an essential note: intentional community may not be ideal, but life without community is more dangerous than life with it imperfectly. We should not await the revival of functional bonds in order to make loving contact with those we are explicitly called to love.)

When multiple families bridge the practical and functional gap, connected in economic dependency included, then we arrive at that noble ideal of the village, that beautiful yet practical integration in a place of religion, work, and festivity.

The romance of the village ideal haunts us, the integration of place, craft, community, and religion. The heartbeat of a true village was the Church, surrounded by the craftsman and then the farmer. Or to put it in different words, the heartbeat was God, roof, and food. That might sound like some bare-bones living, but nothing else is needed for a good party (as in a bout of true festivity), so I would be grateful to have that nearby. The village is a conservative ideal because it contains a web of life that is worth conserving in its tangibility, such as soil and architecture, and in its intangible value, such as tradition and culture.

More and more we see corporations and organizations attempting to assume within themselves the life of a village, fulfilling broader human needs. Large companies, for example, might read and discuss all sorts of books about being a "tribe" at work, cultivating the virtues that belong to actual community. There's a logic and goodness here, because they may be recognizing the true void that exists in their people's lives. But a village is made up not just of people that work for one entity; it is composed of differing ages, families, and generally a bond created in a commitment to a place, not in a shared company-centric goal.

"Company culture," because it is created and exists within the context of a particular company, can mimic and imitate culture—even filling some truly human needs for it. Still, it is incomplete and artificial. It is good for us to think of our fellow workers "like a family," as good companies surely do. But we should never confuse them with a real family. Work always has the reality of servility and utility in it. This is not necessarily bad. You can fire an employee; you can't fire a spouse or neighbor.

IV. Who's My Neighbor?

Fathers engaged in local economics are also a bit more on display with their virtues and vices, unable to live a double life at work or home. A man known to be a Christian very well should be expected to be just and fair in his dealings. St. John the Baptist warned the common man about his local and economic dealings. The people asked him what they should do to bear the "fruits of repentance," signs of submission to God and a turning from sin. He gave three answers, all of which were matters of concern for men in a local place—possessions, community needs, taxes, authority, and pay:

> "What should we do then?" the crowd asked. John answered, "Anyone who has two shirts should share with the one who has none, and anyone who has food should do the same." Even tax collectors came to be baptized. "Teacher," they asked, "what should we do?" "Don't collect any more than you are required to," he told them. Then some soldiers asked him, "And what should we do?" He replied, "Don't extort money and don't accuse people falsely—be content with your pay." (Luke 3:10–14, NIV)

Social justice, as understood in the Catholic heart, is not some abstract do-gooderism. It relates to the charity we have in our heart toward our neighbor and their clear needs, such as needing a coat. And, strictly speaking, what St. John the Baptist (and much of Catholic social thought) calls us to is not "charity" at all. It's justice. Not collecting more taxes than are owed isn't generosity; it's the basics of right and wrong. It would be our Lord that would call men to lay their lives down for friend and neighbor. It was John that called them to get square with them first to make love possible. Similarly, it is local economics that call a man to "get square" with his neighbor, bringing considerations of justice and rights closer to home and out of the clouds.

It is no secret that our society has grown lonely and isolated, but men and fathers seem to have a unique cross in this matter, which is at least partly to blame in their *lack* of associations. Men, in their practicality, can easily unite over practical matters, but guilds in the past—at least, those born explicitly from Catholic hearts—had also as their object the impractical need of friendship and love. These local associations are born from local care and work, and they are also well suited to answer for disasters and needs, as we see in local fire departments and food banks. They also advance the trades and provide training to ensure that the next generation is in continuity with what preceded them.

It is worth noting that in the past, these guilds were also the patrons of local devotions and the feast days associated with them. But they also answered other human needs for relationship. We think today of medieval guilds in their focus on craft, which was there, such as guilds of blacksmiths or bakers. Yet, as Gervase Rosser has shown in *The Art of Solidarity in the Middle Ages*, guilds also explicitly called for a code of life that went beyond material needs into human and spiritual ones. "The fostering of affection amongst the members was a universally expressed goal of the fraternities." A canon for the York Paternoster guild in England, for example, took to itself reconciling brothers outside of civil courts as a witness to the power of Christian community:

> It is forbidden that any brother of the guild shall, in the belief that he will have help from his brethren, be forward in getting into a lawsuit of quarrel ... upon pain of losing all help and friendship, or any relief, from the guild.

The guild of St. Catherine near Cambridge had as a canon that "each brother ... of the guild should love one another with all the zeal of which they are capable."

Proponents of localism and the economy of the home (and salvation for that matter), therefore, don't just relate a father back to his community for the sake of the practical needs alone—though they begin there—but in true Christian spirit seek to go beyond to the good of man in both body and soul.

V. Paths Forward, Together

I can hear the argument: that my air conditioning and frozen Costco goods prove me to be a hypocrite—even if it's my *local* Costco. Worse still, I work in an administrative role with a non-profit called Fraternus, a work I do through phone and computer. I love Fraternus because it cultivates the local fraternal bonds of men and initiates the next generation. Yet the day-to-day of the work is hard to share with my family and has little impact on my neighbor outside of paying a salary I spend locally. In true dad-fashion, let's get practical about the temptation to dismiss localism as a romantic ideal that isn't fully lived and is, therefore, dismissible.

First, I would point out that "hypocrisy always brings tribute to the strength of an idea." (That formulation I also borrow from Gervase Rosser.) Hypocrites annoy because of the weakness of their life, not the weakness of their ideals. In these cases, however,

I think charges of hypocrisy rest more in a fear to question the status quo, or a fear of not being grateful enough to technological advances, which is not the true issue of localism. Belloc makes the case in *The Servile State* that technological advances do not require consolidated power to exist. In fact, it is observed today that many advances in tech seem to be slowing down as fewer companies own larger shares of the market.

Secondly, most men today find their way toward delocalized jobs not by choice or inheritance but by a force of coercion so strong it takes a holy version of Nietzsche's Übermensch to resist it. Even so, many men do slowly realize, by degrees, the necessity of localism for human flourishing, often as their family grows and seeks a more settled and natural state. Yet even if men must maintain their economic bindings to globalism, their dedication to spending, acting, and caring locally is not therefore meaningless, trivial, or dismissible. As they say, the perfect is no enemy of the good. It is better to start living right than shrug at the difficulty of it.

Third, localized work and economy is not dead. We're not talking unworkable romance at all. In fact, these people are all around us. Dismissing them proves a certain aloofness to reality, with a touch of arrogance. You can't export the job of a plumber to China, and it's a good paying job that has a much more afford-able entry path than many other careers. Local work still exists, is accessible, and is capable of rooting and supporting a family. And these men deserve our respect and patronage.

VI. My Farm

In closing, I can look through a lived lens, because my family is engaged locally by living on a farm. And by "living on a farm," I do not mean we have a few animals and a garden for our own use or for the sake of prepping. I am aware that many "farms" today are not the peasant's last chance but serve as a symbol of social status (which, by the way, artificially inflates land by dislodging value from productivity). We don't do Instagram farming or have goats as backdrop for selfies. Our farm is a micro-dairy, registered and regulated as a commercial dairy, that provides for the needs of my family and serves as a humanizing and functional bridge to our local place. We grow food and sell it. Without the local economy it provides for, I don't know how I, as a father, would cultivate such a sense of service and love for our neighbors.

There are other ways, I am sure. I just don't have them in hand. In what I have proposed here, I can say quite clearly that the romance of localism is not empty romanticism but the most practical and truest kind. Practical fruitfulness and romance are not exclusionary, as marriage itself proves.

Selling at the farmers' market connects my homeschooled children to the community in a beautiful and practical way, and we understand what we do to be an integration of our family's needs along with our neighbors'. My children are concerned if someone stops at our farm store for milk and we haven't bottled yet. We have cash on hand in the store to help a regularly needy neighbor out. (He might be a mess, but he always pays me back.) We've visited the local wood mill for barn siding and learned that the man that runs it is a literal hero of endurance and love. (He also sells wood cheaper to us because we milk cows, a reasoning hard to grasp unless you've seen functionality depart your community as he has.) We're here when the local sheep farmers need emergency milk for their lambs. (One of those farms is as politically "Left" as I've come across in the country, yet our mutual dependency unites us in common care.) We let those strange fishermen that fish for carp make their bait from our cow manure. (Yes, that's a real thing.) To attract people to our farm store, we carry goods from other farms nearby, and we have built friendships there that would not have grown otherwise. We have farming mentors that help us treat injured cows, cut hay, and make decisions on everything from breeding heifers to planting a new field. Our farm brings us into relationship with these people, and we have an affection for them that has its roots in our locally shared cares. Talking about the weather with them is not the passing of time but a matter of shared concern and connection.

This connection strengthens my family's institutional rootedness here and with each other. We're here in a place that is growing to need us as we grow to need it. As the farm grows, we grow as a family in our mutual need for one another. I was able to go meet Wendell Berry at a conference only when my son was capable enough to run the farm, milking the cows alone by age nine—a fact that tickled Berry visibly when we spoke. As much as I like to think that my interpersonal skills and care for home and community would make such bonds possible, I have witnessed the power of natural economy—of localism—do what true ideas alone could not.

The natural economy of man is formed when his means of providing are secure in the form of productive property—which is not just arable land in farming but also home-based craft and trades. It is ordered and holy when he is able to hold and cultivate that possession as his own (private property) and have the security that comes with it for the sake of those he cares for (his family and community). Local and stable bonds are especially maintained by men and fathers, and these bonds matter more than material security. They're sources of family integration and communal harmony. Localism will never make inroads if fathers are not on board.

Local economic reality is no bumper sticker idealism—at least, it won't be that when dad is dedicated to it. It is the true, authentic, and natural life of man as husband, which has roots in the word "house bound," as in bound to a home and a home to him. It is also related to the word husbandry, the care of creatures in and around a home for the sake of the home. This life brings men in contact with their local place and its people, and it creates and protects the communal life of man, which is not a superfluous part of his life but a source of it. That which removes man from his home and place, therefore, is something we should resist.

All Freedom Is Local

ANTHONY ESOLEN

I wish that Catholics who have "social teaching" on their lips
would begin to consider what a genuine society is, and what it
is for, and not think of it merely as an agglomeration of people
who happen to live within certain wide-flung political boundaries.
When I think about what is social, the engines of the contemporary welfare state do not come to mind, whether those engines do
good work or bad. The truly social warms my heart, though I am
shy by nature and not the most sociable of persons, and therefore
I want people to do more things together, and more important
things, in their bulky bodily persons, than they commonly do
now. Whether that welfare state makes the sociable less likely, or
in what kinds of places and under what conditions it might do so,
I leave to others to discern, as it requires a peculiar attention to
precise details that might distinguish a thousand-year-old village
in Sweden from a subdivision sprouting up near the intersection
of two American interstate highways. For the policies of a welfare
state tend to abstraction and indifference to persons and their
local ways of life.

Be that as it may, our Church is for persons, not agglomerations
of human material, and we would do well to keep it in mind as

we consider what is actually good for people, what does good for heart and mind and soul and body. I am not speaking here of such necessities as food and medical care. I am speaking of other things no less necessary, but easier in our time to forget, because we can do without them and still lug our bodies from place to place; we live, but we do not live well, or even as fully human beings. One of those things is freedom, which I think is the very air in which the social flourishes.

We have been taught to consider it otherwise, as if freedom were at cross purposes with the social, either because the social, improperly understood, takes a third to a half of what I earn or because freedom, improperly understood, is in defiance of the moral claims of others. Let us not be deceived. I have long thought about the progressive cramping and reduction of modern life, accompanied and enabled by developments in technology and accompanied and perhaps necessitated by the only two or three ways in which we can plausibly begin to assert that we enjoy more liberty than we did before. We can go more places. We have—perhaps—a wider range of livelihoods to choose from; but when I think of the tailors, shoemakers, grocers, miners, and dairymen of my depressed hometown in Pennsylvania when I was a boy, I hedge. We certainly are more licentious by far in our sexual habits, a license that seems to result not in merriment, not in any greater gratitude of each sex for the other, and obviously not in the proliferation of marriage and any increase in its influence over every feature of our social and political lives, but in sullenness, mutual distrust, and loneliness.

I think that a definition of freedom that neglects freedom's inner spirit and ultimate end—a definition that is fundamentally negative, that is, that freedom implies a dispensation from the controlling demands or oversight of others—is inadequate, and it is a symptom of our malady that we no longer trouble to ask those larger questions of inherent nature and goal. Still, even by that narrow and feeble definition, it seems unquestionable that we are less free than people in previous generations were—and that we are therefore less social.

Let us suppose you have a legal system that guarantees immunity from the law for anything you please to do in the strictly private sphere, so long as you are not killing someone, beating him up, setting his house on fire, or stealing his goods. Now suppose that in that same land you are afraid to walk alone when the sun is down, and suppose that children are hustled and harried from pillar to post, always under the watchful eye of adults, and suppose that almost the only things you can buy are those that have come from factories far away, made without the distinctive touch of any particular human maker, and suppose that a nearly impassable forest of codes and regulations makes it practically impossible for you to set up any kind of shop, unless you have plenty of money up front or you are willing and able to go deeply into debt. Freedom, really?

Let's consider a few examples. For the sake of argument, we'll agree that whatever else it is or does, human freedom implies an openness to spontaneity, whimsy, risk, the curiosity of individual inclinations, and a sort of carefree capacity for people to get together to form their own informal groups with their own aims and habits. What do we make, then, of the sight of children riding a bus to a consolidated public school too far from home for them to walk to, too plainly separate from whatever common life remains on the town streets to be a daily part of the larger lives of a wide variety of people of all ages, and, of course, too large and too "professional" to be answerable to the parents, let alone to take from them any creative direction? It is standardized: it hardly varies from Maine to California, as anyone who has taught their best products in college—I use the word "products" advisedly—can readily tell, as you can dependably predict which false things they have been taught, and which vast fields of human enterprise they know nothing of at all. The ride there is as cramped and troublesome in late summer as in the dead of winter. The ride admits of no choice; and the stops are regular, drearily regular, day after day, year after year, world without end. Bus and school thus go together. You take a machine to get to and from a machine. Now imagine children *not riding a bus to school.*

If the Puritan is a man who fears that someone, somewhere, may be enjoying himself, the enemy of freedom is a man who fears, if I may use the single case as representative of all, that children are walking home from school. What may they be doing? What may they not be doing? I will suggest what I myself have done or seen. They may stop at the drug store or the lunch counter. They may stop at the barber's for a haircut. They may go to the ballfield to play. They may go to a classmate's house. They may stray off into the woods, just because it is fun to tramp the hills and look for whatever turns up. They may swarm over the back streets. They may go down by the river, to check the fish. While they are doing these things, they are growing, not just in muscle and bone but in initiative and in sociality. And these latter things are far too unpredictable to be fostered in the severely controlled environment of the school. Nor can they be mandated by organs and machines of government generally. Things beyond a human scale, especially when the human beings are but children, inevitably tend toward anonymity, and the best they can do for us is to clear some ground for the real stuff of human life and then, quickly and humbly, get out of the way. But that would require a tact and a humility that such enterprises by their very nature cannot possess. They are pile drivers, when man more often needs a hammer, or a bat and ball, or a sheet of paper and a pen, or a small gauge rifle and a forest full of game.

Such a life for children requires thriving neighborhoods—in city or town or country, for the life principle, the blood, is the same—in which everyone knows everyone else by sight or by name, and that in turn requires what Chesterton called the adventure of domesticity. Each home, after all, is like a little kingdom with its own peculiar laws, its whimsical feast days, its kindred kingdoms and allies, and its traditions hard to translate from one home to another; even the family dog takes on the character of a servant of the manor, regarding, with an air of canine superiority, the ways of the lesser people next door. The flight from the home is the flight from a place where you may do as you please, into standardization and routine; from being king or queen, prince or princess, to the servility of whichever narrow role you assume when you sell yourself in the labor market. To the extent that school "socializes" children, it but trains them to expect such servility and to regard it as the height of human achievement, so long as it comes with a title and a fair amount of money, most of which evaporates. For the life of servility costs dearly. Smaller households, and innumerable single people whose lives are bound to the routine of school and college and debt and work, raise the cost of housing even as they empty the neighborhood of people who will regularly meet one another and talk and play and do the dozens of other things that ordinary people used to do.

I may say, taking a different but similar direction, that the enemy of freedom is someone who cannot believe that a boy and girl are holding hands on their way to the miniature golf course and *are not* sleeping together. Indeed the likelihoods are in inverse relation. The more of an ordinary and strangely cheerless thing it is for them to be sleeping together, the less likely you are to see them blushing with pleasure as they hold hands in public. Imagine a world in which the presumption of innocence makes a wide variety of innocent and love-affirming pleasures conceivable. The boy asks the girl if she wants to go with him—where? To the bowling alley, to the diner, to a movie that even children can attend, to one of the six or seven dances that weekend within ten miles of where they live, to the family-owned lake with its concession stand and arcade, to a local band concert, to the basketball game, to the ice skating rink, to the pond to fish, to the amateur playhouse, or just to his home for supper.

And here I find fault with my fellow Catholics who will not see what is staring them in the face, and that is that the commandments that are guardrails against illicit sexual activity are also hedgerows and fences, and foul lines for the ballfield, and sidewalks and common grounds where people can play without fear of being run over. The domestic life I am describing has solid and child-rich and widespread marriage at its heart, a culture of marriage, that is to say, a culture, properly speaking, that has not been sapped by perverse and life-denying presumptions, prime among which is that one's body is one's own to dispose of at will. Or is that a tad too social for us to consider?

I know, of course, that there are plenty of contributory organs of standardization, routine, and the evacuation of social life. But we do not do a good job of resisting them. "We gave you a nation to be free in," I imagine one of our founders saying, as he looks at the empty landscape of human life, "and this is all you made of it?" And then I imagine an old prelate of the Church, one who understands in a most human way why we teach what we teach, replying, "And how did you think they would do, when you helped them to forget what freedom was for?" At which I myself might turn to a current prelate, and say, "We have done badly. Perhaps now we should return to created reality and first principles, before we even begin to argue about general measures to be undertaken in a nation of more than three hundred million people."

The Mere Poetry of Place

William Edmund Fahey III

Lectrix. Was it here? I believe my brother met you once. Was it here?

Scriptor. I can't recall, but you seem familiar. Is he like you?

Lectrix. I haven't seen him for a while. People said we were similar.

Scriptor. I might have met him. Where do you live? Where is your family from?

Lectrix. No place. That's odd you think those are connected—where someone is from and where they live. Don't people move around a lot? I mean, you're *from* wherever you're *from*, but that's just one of a series of prepositions—"from," "in," "at," "to" ... the place you're from is always changing. *From*'s just the past.

Scriptor. Some prepositions might be more important than others when it comes to the matter of who a person is and what he or she knows.

Lectrix. Like I said, people move around a lot. "From" is just a preposition.

Scriptor. Perhaps, but people are always from someplace. Place is essential. Even if a person is unfortunate enough not to have a place from which he comes, he still *is* someplace, he *lives* someplace. Drop the preposition if you like. Think about the verbs.

LECTRIX. Yes, that's my point. The world is always changing. People change. Places change. Big deal. And why do you say, "unfortunate?" What is so unfortunate about moving around—doesn't moving around broaden experience? Doesn't it lead to enlarged sympathies and a better understanding of humans and the world? That's what I was told in school.

SCRIPTOR. Well, I don't want to condemn every empire or every cosmopolitan soul, but somehow, I wouldn't say that moving around a lot necessarily leads to good things. And I don't want to look down upon every nomadic group, not at all, but modern nomads don't seem to have a way of life. More often than not, they're shuttlecocks to whim and economic pressure.

LECTRIX. I'm not sure what that means, but moving is better than being stuck.

SCRIPTOR. What do you mean?

LECTRIX. It's better not being stuck in one place. Just one place, all the time. No variation. No change. Nothing. That's not life. Life is change.

SCRIPTOR. "Even in a country you know by heart
  It's hard to go the same way twice.
  The life of the going changes."

LECTRIX. What is that?

SCRIPTOR. Part of a poem by a fellow named ...

LECTRIX. What is the point of poem right now?

SCRIPTOR. I think I *did* meet your brother once.

LECTRIX. I thought we were talking about living and moving, and where I'm from or not from.

SCRIPTOR. Well, I find that poetry helps make things more concrete, vivid, moving. Do you know the poem "The Beautiful Changes," or maybe "Paterson"?

LECTRIX. Moving? How about clarity? I don't need that kind of moving. Look, what are we talking about? Where I'm from?

SCRIPTOR. The subject, if you wish to proceed this way for a while, is localism.

LECTRIX. Oh, an -ism word. Now we're talking. I like politics and economics.

SCRIPTOR. Yes, I definitely met your brother. Look, the muse tells me that our subject is "localism." There, I have made it official for you by putting it in quotation marks. Are you interested? Clearly, you *are*, or you wouldn't be here. He chose to be here and, I see, you're staying as well.

LECTRIX. Alright, I'm a little intrigued. So what? Was he really here?

SCRIPTOR. It's interesting what you just did. In a little way you chose to remain rather than move on to something else. That's all.

LECTRIX. If "localism" is about this issue of *where* I am *from* or whether or not I should even worry about the issue, sure, let's go. Teach me something. But I should say from the start, I don't like poetry. Can we start with clarity? Can you define your terms?

SCRIPTOR. Define "localism"? If you wish. I prefer descriptions (I feel somehow that I have been here before). Yes, if you like, I can throw out some definitions.

LECTRIX. Yes, *then* we can get somewhere. Otherwise, well ... it's like poetry—we're just sitting here, blabbing happy-clappy stuff.

SCRIPTOR. Localism is the heart's attachment to a particular geographic place, limited in scope, that assists in normal human happiness.

LECTRIX. Okay. I'm with you. I went to Venice, Italy, once on this trip. It reminded me a little of Miami, but cooler because it was old ... also like Charleston or Santa Fe—ever been there?

I went during Spring Break when I was in college. So classy. Though a little stuffy, I thought. Still, there was something about it and some of those other cities. You've won me over. I like visiting beautiful places. I'm a localist.

SCRIPTOR. I don't think you are a localist yet, but you desire to be.

LECTRIX. But I felt happy when I was in those places . . . and sometimes, I look at the pictures on my phone. That makes me smile.

SCRIPTOR. That's happiness? Answer that one honestly—it's just us. Are you happy?

LECTRIX. So why am I not a localist? What's missing? I'd love to know.

SCRIPTOR. Do you have abiding love for Venice?

LECTRIX. What does that even mean?

SCRIPTOR. Would you give up a higher paying job for it? Would you suffer for it? Do you feel like you would still belong to it, even if you lived on the far side of the world? Is it hard to think of *yourself* without thinking of *that place*. . .? No, I didn't think so. So what I mean by "the heart's attachment" is abiding love. Yet you can't love what you don't know. So I would add something to my definition—which, recall, you are forcing upon me. I'd rather just describe it or write a play about it.

LECTRIX. Go on.

SCRIPTOR. I would add, localism rests upon love and knowledge formed chiefly around three things: first, shared memory. Second, knowledge of the land. Third, familiarity with the poetic vision of the land, history, and people.

LECTRIX. I am lost. Shared memory . . . land . . . poetic vision. Oh, my . . .

SCRIPTOR. You're the one clamoring for definitions.

LECTRIX. Let's start with remembering. You actually said collective remembering. Is that some kind of socialist program or psychological thing?

SCRIPTOR. Well, I said shared memory. What do I mean? I mean that the person does not simply and only remember the place, but the place, or the people of the place, remembers the person. And that the two together—the person's and the community's remembrance—define one another.

LECTRIX. I am lost.

SCRIPTOR. This is what comes of definitions. How about a story? Once upon a time, I moved to a place. I knew the land in a general way, and the history in a general way. I liked the look of the land. I bought an old house in the place—a house that had been built centuries ago by a very, very distant ancestor. When I moved to that place, ordinary people—craftsmen, locals of many generations—knew me ... though they had never met me. They knew me because they could place me in a vast story of folks from that land. When I gave them a brief sketch of my genealogy, they gave back to me a detailed context of people, land, and history. I was known more than I knew. They knew my people, my ancestors, without having met me, but having met me, now I was placed and remembered into a community.

LECTRIX. Still lost.

SCRIPTOR. Look, I was sitting in the kitchen of my little cottage. My children knew I loved the cottage because in the eighteenth century, the land was settled by very distant relatives. The man who knows everything about the neighborhood—who also had plowed my drive—was stopping by. My children had been baiting me to say something and had been joshing with me about my "cousins" in the area. When he came by, I asked him, "What sort of relation are you to the folks who lived here before?" I knew they shared last names, but I did not know their history or connections. He told me that the previous owners and he were first cousins, and he told a few colorful stories. And then he paused, and said, "You're a cousin, too, I understand."

He knew that I had an interest in genealogy and that I had already shared this with the previous owners. "Well," I said, "I don't want to overplay that. Sure. We are related to a man name Ambrose Bowdon who was born in 1585, his son is your great grandfather by about ten generations. His daughter is my great grandmother." I was proud of my knowledge but thought, not without a little pride, that I was a bit condescending with certain details of my research. He looked at me long and then said, "Well, then, your people all came up from Cape Elizabeth area." And then, standing with his arms on his hips, he began to recite something that almost seemed like a poem, naming the locations of places on the coast of Maine by ancient names that I thought only historians knew.

My stiff, newly won antiquarianism collapsed before his deep and living antiquarianism. He could name my ancestors and tell me in detail where they lived. He placed me. Knowing the land and the people of the land, he situated me and named me a cousin, with a little quiet affection, I believe.

LECTRIX. Wild. Weird maybe. But that can't happen with normal people, I mean ...

SCRIPTOR. I know what you mean. But I think it can happen more than you realize. And it will happen if people ever settle down and let it. And by the way, that's a given in our little ramble toward a definition: You eventually have to settle. But look, I will concede that my situation is a little longer in history than some others. Still, everyone can grow into a region and place if they learn parts of its history and customs and allow themselves to become remembered into the history.

LECTRIX. That's a strange expression. "Remembered into the history."

SCRIPTOR. Well, I can think of no better. I mean more than some-one thinking about "becoming a local" or calling themselves a local because they "buy local" or wear a baseball cap from a local shop. I don't think you can just will your way into a place, any more than you can buy your way in. You need time and experiences, and other people need to experience you and make a claim on you.

LECTRIX. I don't know that I want to be claimed or known.

SCRIPTOR. Oh, I think you do. I think everyone does. They may be frightened by that. Deep knowledge of ourselves known by other people.... Intimacy is always intimidating. But we all desire it, even when we come as strangers "out of the woods, worn out upon the trail." Maybe especially, then.

LECTRIX. Who comes out of the woods?

SCRIPTOR. More poetry, Robert Frost. What I mean is that there is a deep desire to be known, included, loved—all those are related.

LECTRIX. Like FOMO?

SCRIPTOR. What?

LECTRIX. Fear of missing out.

SCRIPTOR. Yes. Perhaps also "fear of not being missed."

LECTRIX. F-O-N-B-M.... Doesn't work.

SCRIPTOR. Do you like knowing people missed you?... Yes. I thought so. If you have ever been in love, you have a sense of what I mean.

LECTRIX. Let's stick with defining things. I like boundaries. About this "land" business, how do you know how to limit your con-cept? What is local and what is beyond local?

SCRIPTOR. I would say that the local, as I mean it, is a region too large to exhaust in a lifetime of exploration, but too small not to try.

LECTRIX. That sounds like a jingle for some kind of vacation land. Why do we even need this idea of land? Let's just say, I get what you mean about being remembered and remembering folks, and being loved and all, as part of being happy. . . . I get it, but why is all that necessarily attached to land? Specific land? Why can't I have a friend group online? In fact, I do. A bunch. Those seem like communities.

SCRIPTOR. They may be a kind of community. I'm not arguing for or against true sentiments toward people organized around some idea or common interest. What I'm trying to do is describe a deep human impulse: The desire to be known and loved in a specific place that is also loved.

LECTRIX. All right. But people come and go. Our world isn't stable. I have friends from college or places I once worked. I see them now and again. We talk. What is wrong with that?

SCRIPTOR. Nothing. Necessarily. But I am reminded of these words:

We spake of many a vanished scene,
    Of what we once had thought and said,
Of what had been, and might have been,
    And who was changed, and who was dead;

And all that fills the hearts of friends,
    When first they feel, with secret pain,
Their lives henceforth have separate ends,
    And never can be one again.

LECTRIX. Yes.

SCRIPTOR. Yes? . . . You're quiet now.

LECTRIX. I was just thinking about that line, that part — "with secret pain" and . . . someone I knew, still know. If you don't live together, in the same place, I mean, is that the way it always goes? Living "separate ends"?

SCRIPTOR. No, I don't think so. I'll tell you something else, I think. I think you can live *in the same place* with someone and have separate ends. That's harder still.

LECTRIX. Yes, exactly. There you go. What does place matter, then?

SCRIPTOR. No, consider it. Why do you agree that it's harder when you live in the same place with someone? You *do* agree?

LECTRIX. Alright. Fair enough. Living nearby people may deepen feelings. It doesn't make feelings happen the right way, but if the feelings are there, maybe it does something.

SCRIPTOR. Yes. It fixes them.

LECTRIX. Look, I accept that being in a place with other people makes a difference, but we can't love all the people we are always with, and we can't always be in the places with the people we love. Right? I don't see how this localism thing works.

SCRIPTOR. "Rest where you chose to be."

LECTRIX. What?

SCRIPTOR. "Rest where you chose to be." A poem again. It's the end of a poem by Robert P. Tristram Coffin. You might find it a bit sad. The last stanzas go:

Now on the island where you found
Wild strawberries and love
You lie in the graveyard of your choice,
And the sea winds blow above.

Deer stare at the tinkling cows;
Rest, where you chose to be.
The high fog comes in over the hill
With grey eternity.

It may not be the best of poems as the critics would have it. Coffin may not be the best poet, but he comes from my part of the world. And what's more, he understands.

LECTRIX. Understands what?

SCRIPTOR. Understands a very important thing. Something that you feel. Worded as a question, it would be "How do I become part of a place, if I must be accepted, or remembered?" Part of the answer lies in something maybe I seemed to say initially was not possible—that you can *will* yourself into a place. I still contend that. The poet says, "where you chose to be." "Chose" and "choice" are interesting words. In their roots, they actually mean "to try" or "to taste" and "to enjoy." Tie all those together. The localist might be blessed to be born and live and die in a single place, but he may choose the place, or be chosen by the place. And then he may settle because he finds his joy in that place. He tries it, and he decides it's a good place to die.

LECTRIX. Back to death.

SCRIPTOR. Coffin—that's a funny name given what we're talking about—has another poem you should hear. It opens:

Summer people wonder why the best
Hilltops looking out here on the sea
Are taken up by people gone to rest;
The graveyards spoil the sightliest property,
And that, they hold, is poor economy.

LECTRIX. I think I agree with whomever these "summer people" are. They sound less morbid than this Coffin fellow. Though that poem seems more funny than sad. But what's the story with graves? Isn't there a point to those people questioning why graves should be so prominent?

SCRIPTOR. It is a very good thing to wonder over—the question of graves and tomb memorials. It's good to think about the one direction everyone is going—localists or globalists all—toward their end. Think upon that and it might help set things in order.

LECTRIX. Life's short and all that?

SCRIPTOR. Life's as short or long as a piece of string. I am less concerned about the quantity of time. Time is. What I mean is that it is good to think over what to do with time—the content and quality of it. That's the bit on choosing a good life. Trying it. Tombstones are markers from the past of a place. And they give voice to the people of the place, who ask questions to those not yet in the ground. And they ask, "What did you do with time while you were in this place?" I think that's why they are neglected, hidden, destroyed these days—they stir up dark thoughts.

LECTRIX. What do you mean ... thoughts about death?

SCRIPTOR. Yes, and more, about life. They raise the issues of place, of memory, of loyalties and loves. Gravestones ask how you are living.

LECTRIX. Can we stop with the poems and tombstones? Maybe you're right. I can't even picture where my own family is buried because I don't know.... It's not that I don't appreciate ... something about those poems. It's just I feel they raise emotions and questions that I'm not ready for.

SCRIPTOR. Poetry is good at that. Not so good at definitions.

LECTRIX. That reminds me, poetry was part of your definition.

SCRIPTOR. *Forced* definition, but yes. I never really got to the bones of what I wanted to say about land ... I wanted to talk about geology, and watersheds, and flora and fauna, and ...

LECTRIX. Poetry. You think it's connected to place?

SCRIPTOR. Well, yes. I don't think all poems need be about place, more—maybe most—aren't explicitly about place. I do think the greatness of a poet is more than his technical abilities or what he has read. He needs to be firmly rooted in a place, a place that can inform and nourish his powers of thought. It's the foundational bond that marries his musical impulse to his love of words. Those spring from a knowing love of place. There is an old poem that starts,

As you came from the holy land
Of Walsinghame,
Met you not with my true love,
By the way you came?

Hundreds of songs and ballads deal with this theme of missing your sweetheart, but how impoverished the words would become if the poet's holy land were not named. It would just remain an abstraction, and abstract things are not loved. That particularity—Walsinghame—is not just a bit from a traveler's atlas, it brings the experiences that follow to the very soil of a place. It grounds the experience. Even if you can't place it on a map, you just know that such concreteness reveals things deeply felt and known. But as I say, poems need not all be about place, and certainly the theme of a poem is rarely just "place."

LECTRIX. Interesting, but you're straying just a bit from *our theme*.

SCRIPTOR. Fair enough. What I said was something like localism rested upon a familiarity with the poetic vision of the land, history, and the people. While I am not always keen on definitions, I am keen on words. "Poetic vision" would contain more than the word "poetry" does. Please don't ask me to define it.

LECTRIX. Please, do try.

SCRIPTOR. Poetry is a spontaneous overflow of powerful feelings.

LECTRIX. Huh? Yeah, right. And so is getting frustrated or falling for someone. That definition is out there.

SCRIPTOR. Alright. Poetry is a word that means, from its deepest roots, an act of verbal making, the art of communicating a vision of reality. It relies on wisely arranged words and sounds and a sense of music. Poetic things are patterns of words that move us to understand human experience and reality. They draw us to the eternal freshness of the truth through their disciplined little dramas or images.

LECTRIX. Stop. So perhaps just explain the main point here—why does localism, knowing and loving a place, require the "poetic"?

SCRIPTOR. That is a very good question. I sense an answer, but I will admit, I am only moving toward it—with you and thanks to you.

LECTRIX. Well, give me a poem, then. I know, you're thinking "she doesn't like poetry." Maybe I don't, but maybe I think you do. So here we are, and I'm asking because you like the stuff, and it helps you to explain things to me, and I appreciate you doing that. So give me a poem.

SCRIPTOR. This is the poem . . .

LECTRIX. What is?

SCRIPTOR. That is the title and first line. It's another one by Coffin:

This is the poem, this is Maine;
Sunlight on all things like frost,
Eternity at the end of the lane,
A garden the deer have always crossed.

Woods that come down to the waves,
Pine boughs brushing the apple tree,
Cool white houses, high white graves,
And a man rowing up the sea.

Sweetfern growing in the corn,
The mountain on the whitecapped tide
A buck that feeds with slender horn
By the lamb's white gentle side.

The silver fish under the floor,
Lamps and light houses at night,
The secret and sudden door
That opens dark in a hill of light.

Hot spruces and cool mussel shells,
Tame and friendly bells in under
Necks of cows and the wild bells
Rung by waves white with sea thunder.

A coast like columns fluted clean
Where common men go like winged things,
Single forever, on paths that lean
Under a sky alive with wings.

LECTRIX. Well, I can't say I understand it all—especially that part about silver fish. Sounds odd. But parts were quite ... I don't know.

SCRIPTOR. Moving?

LECTRIX. Yes, definitely moving ... oh, I see. Okay. I see. Alright, I understand a little better. Maybe clarity and moving someone's emotions can be related. Anyway, I can see why you like the poem. It does conjure up a place. And clearly this Coffin seems to share this love and knowledge we've been talking about.

SCRIPTOR. Yes. And frankly, that isn't the world's finest poem, but it is filled—just as you say—with love and knowledge, which, when true, are rather fixed together. Even the silver fish can be understood as part of a love of the place. When you love, you understand things honestly, even what is initially ugly—well, it's clearly part of his knowledge, experience, and love of his home in Maine.

LECTRIX. But I am not from that place. I'm not sure I am from any place. I'm not committing or anything to this localist thing, but let's just say I wanted to be from someplace, to know and love someplace, and ... a person or people in a place. And I wanted to be ...

SCRIPTOR. What? To be happy? What would you do?

LECTRIX. For the sake of argument, let's say so. But I'm a hard case. I don't have a home.

SCRIPTOR. Look, as I started to say at the beginning — everybody comes from someplace. Start with that. Everyone had a home. Everyone has memories of what that was like, of family, maybe not all the best, but ...

LECTRIX. I don't.

SCRIPTOR. What do you mean? These things are true of everyone. You had a home. Home is the people. You came from a ...

LECTRIX. Orphan.

SCRIPTOR. What?

LECTRIX. I'm not like your beautiful stories or these poems. I don't have a place. I never knew a parent. I don't have an origin. I don't know a childhood place or family. I know institutions: the orphanage — residential treatment center — temporary group home, public school, the news, work. Do you understand? There is no memory of Uncle Sal telling stories in the kitchen while Mama and Aunt Maria made pappardelle and the Bolognese sauce. We never went with Grandpa to Elmira to watch the Muckdogs play the Pioneers. I have never rediscovered a cousin and talked around the cracker barrel in rustic Vermont. That stuff's beautiful, if it's real, but I just don't have any lovely origin or memory like that. There is no place to return to. I just want the future. Move forward. Movement. I am an orphan. I was not loved.

SCRIPTOR. Stop. Just slow down. You did have an origin, a place, and love.

LECTRIX. Orphan. Abandoned. No love. No place.

SCRIPTOR. What about your brother?

LECTRIX. Twin apparently. I barely know him now. Maybe he's not my real brother. That's just what we were told. There is no place in my history. My history is abandonment.

SCRIPTOR. Alive. Loved.

LECTRIX. What?

SCRIPTOR. I don't have your experiences or sorrows, but listen. You don't know all the details of your origin. But you know this. Someone made a choice, that choice involved love, and you are alive. You know that. People don't accidentally come into existence. Your mother for whatever reason found herself with you, and that was your place. Maybe you do have a brother. In any case, you were loved because she carried you forward into life. You lived with her for months. You had a place, love, and some knowledge of that love. That place may have been imperfect, filled with hardship, who knows? But it was provided, and you lived with someone who loved you into existence.

LECTRIX. Maybe. Maybe. I do desire it.

SCRIPTOR. Sure. We all do. That's just the way we are designed. All this localism business, it's just the awareness through people and land of something.

LECTRIX. What?

SCRIPTOR. Localism is the awareness of the unseen bonds of love in a place. That awareness takes place across time, and it grows rich with time. Localism involves a stable living and living well—like a good person, I mean—and thinking about life among friends. And like I said, and I mean this, that's just the way we are designed. When you don't have those things—fault or no fault—you are not happy. That doesn't mean you're condemned to be unhappy forever.

LECTRIX. So let's finish this. I want to be happy. But I have no place, no current sense of place … you gave me something a minute ago to think about, about my … origin. But what now? I have no home to go to. I have no "stable living."

SCRIPTOR. Then stop and make one. Or better, stop and accept one.

LECTRIX. What?

SCRIPTOR. It's as easy and as difficult as that. Stop and make a living. Localism — another ugly word for a beautiful thing — takes time, place, and people, all bound together in knowledge, love, and memory. It's already started somewhere. Your goal and your choice are not the creation of an entire place, people, history, folklore, etc. Not at all. Perhaps that is your burden.

LECTRIX. Yeah, I feel like I don't have a choice other than creating a new me, all the time.

SCRIPTOR. Your strongest and best choice is to stop. Think a bit about where to stop. Let it be attractive to you. But then, just stop and get to work. There is no magic formula or comprehensive reading list or online certificate for localism. Fall in love with the concrete, the specific, the real — fall in love with the silverfish as well as "a man rowing up the sea." Our world is pushing you constantly to think of a future made better by being remade — often through things bought. I suggest you stop and accept *gifts* rather than add more purchases to your virtual shopping cart. You are not a corporate algorithm.

LECTRIX. So localism and happiness — it's as simple as stopping, is it?

SCRIPTOR. As I said, it is easy and hard. Look. If you want a plan of action — and I see you do…. Well, do this: Sit someplace and think, "What do I like about this place, this region? Who are the people around here? What's that tree over there? Maybe *this* place is already *the* place." Maybe you are already there. You might need to make another move before you are sitting, thinking, "*this* place." But set your mind to thinking "this place." Take an interest in it.

LECTRIX. You're rambling, vague. That's harsh, maybe. But you're drifting.

SCRIPTOR. No. I don't think I am. *You're* drifting, though you don't want to be, that's why you haven't left. And the fact that you haven't left means … you are already succeeding at finding a place.

LECTRIX. So I sit down and let myself fall in love? That's the trick?

SCRIPTOR. Well, remember, love is generated by knowing a person or place. Happiness is an activity. It doesn't fall from the sky.

LECTRIX. I thought you said I was supposed to expect gifts?

SCRIPTOR. Expectation is active, not passive — you need to look. You need to let yourself adjust to seeing things again. But good sight requires a period of training. You need to work on seeing all the gifts around you.

LECTRIX. So this is the part of the story where I buy my field guide, and learn about flora and fauna, and my history of the region, and join a local bridge club? And then I live happily ever after?

SCRIPTOR. I said it is both hard and easy. Bridge is probably too hard. Go for dominoes. And don't forget the place has to have your own "Hot spruces and cool mussel shells, Tame and friendly bells" and all that. That's the essence of it, but you left out two important things.

LECTRIX. What?

SCRIPTOR. Look for your "man rowing up the sea."

LECTRIX. And?

SCRIPTOR. Read some poems. Will you?

The School of Localism

Then let us pray that come it may,
(As come it will for a' that,)
That Sense and Worth, o'er a' the earth,
Shall bear the gree, an' a' that.

—Robert Burns

It is either one of the comedies or tragedies of the human drama that liberty leads to libertinism—which is no longer liberty, of course, but slavery to self-indulgence. As every Golden Age myth reminds us down the centuries, human culture has a downward trajectory, tending toward collapse. Even in this day and age of security and amenity, the greatest threat to the free world—besides democracy—is the loss of the meaning of freedom. When people are free enough to live as they please, speak their minds, and do what they will (so long as they do no harm as defined by law), they eventually come up with a fresh idea of freedom. But it is in this newer and wilder concept of freedom knowing no bounds, of what purports to make society holy and hardy, that now threatens education, compounding and perpetuating the misunderstanding of freedom.

Localism

Freedom does not grant the license to define freedom. Freedom is not freeform. That much is set firmly in stone and will not admit customization—though the rampant re-definers of the world are hard at it. When something is "free," it is not just a situation of acquisition without payment. What it means to "be free" is not simply action with comfortably distant boundaries. Freedom is actually a thing that requires restriction and comes at great price and with narrow prerogative. What is more, an education that sets people free—a truthful education, a liberal education—not only prepares and disposes men and women to undertake that cost but also to assume the character of a free people within an economy that founds and furthers that freedom. But we are falling fast away from any such society, making such ideas about freedom and education more like dreams and drivel than possibilities and prospects. Even so, amid the boom and bluster of mega-corporations and global business—the "madness of bigness" as G. K. Chesterton called it—the debate over distributism, or localism, is not dead.

Describing distributism, the late Stratford Caldecott wrote that it "can be seen as a practical expression or implication of the Catholic social doctrines of subsidiarity in solidarity, of the common good, and of the family as the best foundation of a healthy civil society." Distributism is both a model and a mindset of communal life and labor that distributes private property on a local level in order to encourage people to assume a palpable and even powerful ownership in the place they live and in what they do as contributors to life in that place. Caldecott goes on to say:

> Distributism is not socialism. It does not suppose that property should be stolen from the rich and given to the poor, or appropriated by the state or by a party representing the people, but rather that legislation should make it

easier for the small property-owner, landowner, tradesman, and shopkeeper to survive, and harder for the tycoon to accumulate so much wealth and power that the former is forced to become a mere employee of the latter, or effectively a wage-slave.

But this model of widespread ownership is so removed from the norm of today that it sounds like a fairytale. Hobbiton is a foolish fantasy to those immured in a galactic Star Wars empire. Ownership of those sprawling markets and commercial monsters that make the world go round and that hang over all like the sky are owned by only a very few organizations that are so large and looming they cannot be encountered in any meaningful way, much less comprehended by the common consumer. One glance, if such a thing is possible, at the investment equity titan Blackstone Group would make even Google blush. And more likely than not, most people haven't even heard of Blackstone—but it owns and leases real estate on a scale that amounts to a planetary power. And though they are not always as obvious as Amazon, these corporations are looming larger in reality and recognition, like the giants that loomed over La Mancha—industrial, supersized enemies of the highest yet humblest human attitudes. Blessed are the meek, after all, for they shall inherit the land.

Regarding that inheritance, G. K. Chesterton wrote in *The Outline of Sanity*:

Property is a point of honour. The true contrary of the word "property" is the word "prostitution." And it is not true that a human being will always sell what is sacred to that sense of self-ownership, whether it be the body or the boundary. A few do it in both cases; and by doing it they always become outcasts. But it is not true that a majority must do it; and anybody who says it is, is ignorant, not of our plans and proposals, not of anybody's visions and ideals, not of distributism or division of capital by this or that process, but of the facts of history and the substance of humanity.

We are all accustomed to this prostitution, this overlordship, and it is a pity since it clashes with the whole of human history, human instinct, and human nature. Yet the closest thing most people get to Chesterton's ideal "three acres and a cow" these days is the drive-thru jingle "I'll have a number three and a milkshake." $7.99 at the window. Billions served. Conveyer-belt consumerism for all. Meanwhile, imaginations that are not yet dull think on the dream of Don Quixote, or the romance of Robin Hood, or the patriotic glory of Sir William Wallace, or the simple sanctity of St. Isidore, who plowed with the angels with a new wistfulness for idealism and independence. A reaction is called for and may even be brewing.

In its origins, distributism is a reaction of renewal or return that gained traction as a thought experiment in the early twentieth century, when thinkers lost faith in grasping governments and proposed turning away from the overreaching power of political parties and programs. They envisioned the polar opposite of the progressive machinations that control the impersonal yet powerful corporate engines of the world as we know it. And we all feel the effects of that about which Hilaire Belloc forewarned when he said, "If we do not restore the Institution of Property we cannot escape restoring the Institution of Slavery; there is no third course."

Distributism invites cooperation together with competition in an enactment of freedom in the freest sense: free to do well and be well, free to realize the unimpeded capacity to achieve the good. To the scandal of a money-centered mentality, freedom has far more to do with personal accountability than a personal accountant. Rather than the bulk of commerce being concentrated under a handful of globalized magnates, distributism calls for the opportunity for normal people to take their lives and labors into their own hands and their own responsibility by means of concrete and dignified occupation. Tangible work with tangible impact and tangible import is rewarding as it imparts a real ownership and real consequences of productivity that affect the quality of life and effect the possibility for long-lost loves – namely, the love of labor and the labor of love.

Without this relation, a spirit of discontent rules over the sphere of work and jobs and careers, and this malady is the consequence of a thoroughly practical perspective on labor and freedom, a shackling spirit that is not unfamiliar in the free world. Freedom in the "land of the free" is labeled as license, which only imprisons when inclinations diverge from the good. This American delusion defines liberty as thinking and acting at will within the parameters of a basic concept of the common good, and getting whatever is wanted – and moreover, or increasingly more often than not, that the government is there to give it. But government handouts and bailouts and corporate control breed lazy entitlement and spawn capitalist kingdoms and socialist systems. They do not promote freedom but slavery. Effort is viewed solely as an instrument to be used to some external effect, and work is simply seen as an investment in productivity, like Orwell's pathetic Boxer and his pathetic mantra, "I must work harder." By this Marxist principle, we live to work, as opposed to a traditional anthropology and Catholic Social Teaching that posit that we work to live. The utilitarian reduction of human action offers a very narrow view of labor, arising from a very narrow view of humanity, and it therefore lacks that vision that brings hope and beatitude.

Distributism is more than another civil doctrine. It is a proportionate civil setting designed for the material and spiritual needs of human beings who are endowed with freedom by God and who must find satisfaction and salvation in the sweat of their brow. Man should enact that freedom in a context that is appropriate to his nature and state. Though lofty in its paradigms, distributism takes seriously what a free people need, proposing and promoting the freedom to own property, conduct business with their community, and raise a family in security. Though idealistic, the ideal and the idea of distributism is not ideological; it is freedom from ideologies that hinder the freedom man possesses and should enjoy. Distributism hinges on philosophy rather than policy: a way of life and of thinking about what life is, and especially about freedom.

Until the kings of the free world become philosophers instead of businessmen, however, the road to distributism will be a rocky one. And even if it made an appearance, much depends on who's doing the distributing. In the meantime, though, the way we come to understand the way the world works and the workings of the world begins in the first school of the family and then is carried on in the schoolroom—and it is in these sanctuaries that people should strive to restore the understanding of human nature, human freedom, and human society. If distributism can, in fact or to some degree, form or reform the social structure of the free man, then what kind of education will prepare him to enter into that freedom? One thing is for certain: it isn't the education at large today, which is burdened by the bristling ideologies and bludgeoning propagandas that engrain subservience to a big-box system. But there is an approach to education that is liberating and more conducive to a liberal civilization, that is, a free civilization.

Education is just as subjugated as the social order it supports, programmed to follow a certain pattern and produce a certain product. As Chesterton said, "The moment men begin to care more for education than for religion, they begin to care more for ambition than for education." The prison of education lies in that it is treated like a science instead of the art that Cardinal Newman called it, which is fundamentally restricting and seems to become even more restricting the more money is cast into its strange furnace. Schools are not research institutions or data mills. They are conservatories of culture. Given the widespread admission of the failure of education, mainstream strategies attempt to solve the problem that our schools are not turning out well turned-out human beings by setting more objectives, creating more diagrams, and making more masterplans for competing in the global economy. Classical and Catholic educators also try to solve the problem of the failure of culture and catechesis with curricula and lesson plans of their own.

Teachers should do everything in their power to resist this perfunctory, utilitarian, and ultimately Gradgrindian approach (read the opening pages of Charles Dickens's *Hard Times*) if the free man is ever to walk and work and worship again. There exists, of course, the reactionary quarters who sense, or even see, the problem but are too timid or tired to break the established traces. These say that schools should return to something like the classics but not the classics; or something like the Catechism, but not the Catechism. The preferred route is a textbook with prepackaged points, lesson plans, and piles of worksheets. Real education, on the contrary, commands: "Go to the source;" and that source is the union of goodness, truth, beauty, tradition, and mystery; not information that is learned only to be forgotten in an automatic existence. The problem in education today is that education is dealt with as a problem instead of as a pleasure, and therein lies the seed of slavery instead of freedom, and the beginning of every person's career as a financial functionary or mindless cog.

According to Ryan Grant, writing on this subject of education and distributism:

> The concept of society has fallen out completely from the school environment, and now it is focused on the needs of the individual only in the sense of what kind of comfortable white collar job he might be able to attain. "What college are you going to?" or "Well, if you want to go to college you need to take these classes." "You could do that but you won't get into a good college." A certain level of excellence and achievement in basic things is necessary for a functioning educational system, but after a certain level of knowledge, which ought to be common to the majority of men in society, the traditional focus of education shifted to what the individual could *do* and educating him in like fashion. He might be apprenticed to a trade and put in a position at a young age to provide for himself when he is older by owning his own labor. Students who did not fall into this category still received a good education in many of the basic arts and sciences so that when he went to university he could enter any of those fields. Our educational system at present, however, is worn out, overtaxed, and underperforming. It is focused on material ends for the purposes of tax contribution and not the eternal end for which every individual himself is journeying.

As Grant concludes, and Pope Pius XI corroborates in his encyclical *Divini Illius Magistri*, education that does not address man's final end is no education at all. Education is not simply a means of getting along in the world, because there is far more to life than making a living. This is a central idea behind distributism, showing, unsurprisingly, that there is some connective tissue between a real education and a real civilization.

Education is a good in itself, not merely an instrument to success. The secret of education is that there is no universal method, manual, system, or program to implement or follow in the formation of human beings. Educators and schools today are accustomed to a highly structured approach to classes, tending toward materials that are very systematic, with a table of contents, an index, and a step-by-step track that moves in a fixed and results-driven manner. But this is not the mode of education—the mode of drawing out, as its etymology suggests. Education happens where there is a free, interpersonal consideration of those works and ideas that are eternal, where a student can experience learning purely on its own merits, without outlines, guides, or textbooks. Education arises from conversation, not from commentaries—from the transmission of experiences and impressions from one person to another. People learn from people, not from programs. The error of today is the emphasis on new-fangled technique and technology and the de-emphasis on old-fashioned teaching, learning, working, and living.

Post-modernity is peppered by scientism, according to an inheritance from Descartes, positing that a mathematical protocol of registering means will produce the truth in every subject—but this algorithmic idea does not belong in a comprehensive educational approach. Education is not an equation of simple utility or action. Learning cannot be programmed. Real teaching is beyond outlines because the teacher must be a necessary and irreplaceable component to the teaching experience. Teachers therefore should not depend on, or be limited by, strictures or structures. Teaching and learning at their best are free from predetermined servile ends, considering those things that can be known and enjoyed for their own sake. Such things are the best things—things that are good, true, and beautiful. Science substitutes the enjoyment of perfection with the enjoyment of investigation, which has its own pleasure, but it is not as high as the pleasure of experiencing, considering, and enjoying. When the object is to analyze and pry apart, looking at component parts and elements and characteristics, the subject is a corpse, not the thing as it truly is—when it is most itself—and poets like Wordsworth and wizards like Gandalf agree.

Like the rhythms and realities that make human society sane, the art of education is not a gnostic acquisition. It is obvious, dealing with basic human interaction and happiness. As an action, it has more to do with trust and doing less well than with systems and scripts and sales. Again, like the culture that arises from the honest interaction of honest men, teaching requires faith, together with an open heart, a good will, a love of subject, and facility in conversation. Teachers should appeal to their students' senses and then let their senses have their way. They should challenge them to approach the material as people, not as programs following a closed system. They should remind them not to worry about arriving at a definite conclusion. They should invite students to enjoy the material with them, talking about what they think, like, and do not like. And they should never hesitate to cultivate intellectual darkness, otherwise known as wonder. They should allow subjects to mingle, using chalk instead of screens, books instead of textbooks, and subjects instead of specimens. Above all, they should trust; for only faith can bring about the culmination of education: the perfection of each person at the hands of another person.

While this idea may be seen as the character of a liberal educa-tion, it is hand in glove with what might be called the character of a "distributist education." An education that forms a person according to the principle of enacting a meaningful place in a recognizable society must hinge first on instilling a sense of what it means to have a labor of love and secondly on how to find that love in labor. Without love, there can be nothing much in labor than the daily grind, from which distributism is the opposite. And without an education that introduces students to a wide distribution of subjects, showing both their integration and integrity, the chances of finding that love in every person's work in the world is diminished.

The type of education that seeks this distribution and experience of subjects is becoming very rare. It is very special precisely because it is not specialized. As it is one of the marks of a liberal education, it is little wonder we see more and more capitalist subjugation in society. But liberal education is, as its name suggests, freeing because it puts the whole world on the horizon, giving a person at least an introduction and even some familiarity with those arts that express the Creation and man's place in that Creation. From mathematics to music, history and humanities, literature and poetry, physics and logic, architecture and philosophy: these are the liberating arts, the disciplines that provide people with a sense of their place on earth and in society, which foster that knowledge and appreciation for the distribution of labor and love.

A liberal education is not simply an archaic or nostalgic kicking about in the dustbin of time but rather a movement toward the highest human freedom, which should find its peak in the religious contemplation of the transcendental realities: namely, the good, the true, and the beautiful—those realities that the gospel teaches will set us free. These arts, ranging from astronomy to biology, awaken the soul to exercise and assert itself to its utmost capacity, and that is the purest type of freedom that any education can provide: the freedom to think and act with conviction, the freedom to know what is lovable and what is not, the freedom to pursue happiness and fulfillment.

If pursued with persistence and patience, the Liberal Arts provide a solid foundation in both the theoretical and the practical. Though these disciplines are not what would be called specialized, they encourage and foster a special spirit of curiosity and confidence—or, as Socrates put it, a wonder that leads on to wisdom. It is in this mode of firsthand, hands-on learning and living that distributism, or the mindset that would make distributism possible, can find foothold and fecundity. The cornerstones of grammar, rhetoric, and logic lay out the way that the mind operates. Arithmetic, geometry, and astronomy turn those minds to the way the world operates. And philosophy and theology, colored with poetry and music, engage our final end, giving people truth and true freedom.

Thus, Plato's dialogue teaches that wisdom begins in wonder, and the freedom of wisdom is best begotten in an education of wonder. Make no mistake: education does seek an end—the conversation is not held simply for its own sake. Socrates loved and pursued wisdom, and wisdom *is* best begotten through wonder. And that is precisely why he asked questions and had conversations. Enjoyment, however, is not about critical questions. The expression for enjoyment in Latin is *fruor*, which also provides the root for fruition, or fruitfulness: that kind of perfection Odysseus praises as he feasts with the noble yet homey Phaeacians. In the end, it is true that the humanities humanize, and if anything is necessary for distributism to work, it is human beings who know what it means to be human.

When people encounter the mystery of the reciprocal dependence of all things, they will embrace that reality in the way they live, and distributism is born of that vision. Education in the

Liberal Arts can bestow that vision by drawing people on toward things that are truly and transcendentally good, true, and beautiful—things that bring healthiness, holiness, and happiness. When people have an identifiable part to play that can be a source of peace and pride in providing for themselves and those around them, we encounter the marriage of a liberal education and the free society of distributism—a society where there is an emphasis on the intellectual freedom to identify the good and the practical freedom to engage and achieve it. Such conditions of freedom are precisely the goal of a distributist philosophy, education, and society.

It is a wonder worth contemplating that a wide knowledge actually lends itself to local endeavor. When education is well rooted in gazing and grasping at the stars, it brings Heaven and earth together with hearts and hands. It chips away at forming people into who they are, encountering their strengths and weaknesses and applying them all to a perfection that is in harmony with the visible and invisible world. This is the type of experiential education that stands to advance the possibilities of distributism as it renders the product-driven, nine-to-five, master-planned life, marketplace mentality pretty vapid, to say the least. That sort of life is not what education is for because education is not simply a training but rather a transformation. And that transformation might elevate into a transfiguration the more men and women enter into the Way, the Truth, and the Life; for in that triumvirate of Three-in-One is freedom—on earth as it is in Heaven. And that freedom is happiness.

We often hear people lament over all the things we have lost in our benighted age of enlightenment. Perhaps the single greatest thing we have lost, though, is the *sense* of what we have lost, or that we have lost anything at all. There once was a time when every man—be he doctor or lawyer, priest or plumber—maintained at least a nodding acquaintance with the likes of Achilles and Caesar and Hamlet. But, alas, for our great supplanting era of wondrous wealth and convenience, it is the best of times, it is the worst of times. The small has, however, historically been able to effect large change, and the return of the Liberal Arts as a distributist David against the corporate Goliath is not impossible, for the devotees of localism must adhere to the Schumacherian principle that small is beautiful and begin the restoration of education, and of culture, in the home, in the local school, in the hometown, and onward to the country. Though such steps will require the reclamation of common sense in the country, which may seem a staggering prospect, but common sense is catching, for happiness is power-ful in its attraction for it is good, which is, as Aristotle says, that which all men desire.

Localism Is Americanism

Matthew Giambrone

When our first child was born, she had big blue eyes, short blonde hair, and a pronounced distributist streak. The blue and the blonde were a lovely surprise (Gregor Mendel had given us to understand that my dark features would be dominant), but it was the distributism that was really striking. We had birthed a creature who was neither a capitalist nor a socialist.

The timing could not have been better. My wife and I had been wondering about our own economic affiliations.

Early in adulthood, if you had asked me mine, I would have said something along the lines of "I'm a capitalist, I guess." I was an American; I cherished my country. And Americans are historically capitalists—it is part of our national identity. It seemed somehow even to rise out of our Judeo-Christian roots: in God and His capitalists we trust. I knew capitalism was all about owning private property: that felt right and natural—I didn't think the government should own everything. Also, I had some entrepreneurial tendencies all my life, starting a business at age thirteen and various others since; capitalism encouraged people to do this sort of thing, to work hard, to build something, to find a path other than government handouts.

On the other hand, capitalism as it actually played out seemed different than the vision. Despite talk from the government and industry about the importance of small businesses like mine, the Bible seemed to be the only place where Goliath wasn't actually in charge—a small number of the capitalists held *de facto* power beyond all measure. While we all had a right to own property, that same small number of people owned a colossal amount of it, while a large number of people owned none. And nothing in this seemed much like the America we hear about in songs and read about on monument placards. It was something else. Yet even with all its faults, it was better than the shackles of socialism. So ... I was a capitalist, I guess?

If you had asked my wife's economic leaning at the time, you probably would have received a more straightforward answer. "I have no idea." The people in college had tried to convince her that she was a socialist. That used to be a word not often heard except in derision (or in Eurasia), but young Americans now embrace it. They thought she should, too, because she cared about the poor. But in real life, versus lecture halls, socialism ends up making things worse for the poor and adding to their numbers. And she came at the whole thing from a Christian perspective, but socialism was all tied up in Marxist ideas that didn't comport.

On the capitalist side, she shared both my patriotism and my concerns. She also felt that something about the very remote way we do capitalism in our modern world was dehumanizing. Home and food and clothing, the fixtures of life, the tools of work and trappings of rest—all the materials of human existence, in fact—are always close to us because, by our physical nature, by our *embodied* nature, we are always close to them. It never felt right to her that the things creating, coloring, and ruling them were not also close to us. Our outsourced, disembodied, click-to-order world is in continuous assault against the truth of what we are.

Where did this leave us? There were only two games in town, and neither seemed worth playing. We were not hardcore capitalists, at least not in the finance capitalism or Silicon-Valley capitalism or spend-your-life-in-meetings-and-traffic-jams sense of the word. But we were not socialists. What were we? We were an economically anchorless, young couple expecting a baby. Thus, it was quite something when she was born a distributist.

By the grace of God, at almost exactly the same time our baby arrived, a book arrived also—and various others to follow (babies and books). We became entranced by the writings of a man named G. K. Chesterton. Here was someone who understood us, better than we did, someone who could perhaps explain us to us.

As early as a century ago, he and his friends made the interesting claim that capitalism and socialism are not much good and the startling claim that capitalism and socialism are not much different. Intriguing, but what did it mean? How could the world's two great economic foes be akin? We had to expand our perspective.

If we ignore for the moment some underlying philosophy and overlaying associations, Chesterton's meaning might boil down to this: Socialism holds that the means of production ought to be centralized in the hands of the state. Capitalism holds that the means of production ought to be centralized in the hands of private owners. But both take for granted the notion that they ought to be centralized at all.

If diagrams are helpful, you can envision a spectrum running from left to right. On one side is *public ownership*, on the other *private ownership*. This was the line my wife and I were trying to navigate, drawn toward the private side, yet never quite feeling satisfied at the destination. But if we now add another line, perpendicular to the first, running from top to bottom, and ranging from centralization to localization, we can begin to envision a more complete field of possibilities. Across the top we have a small number of large centers of power and production—all things big, consolidated, remote. And at the bottom we have a large number of small centers of power and production—those things close, proximate, familial, and human in scope.

It is in this sense that capitalism and socialism are not opposites. They both have the same sort of architecture; they both play in the upper regions of the diagram, centralizing power and operating from the top down. This set off some alarm bells for me. I had experience in the design and analysis of complex systems, and from that work, I knew that highly centralized architectures are fragile: They are top-heavy; they have vulnerable single points of failure; they easily bottleneck; they rely on transmission over long, precarious distances. Things only go well when things go according to plan, which is a silly thing to plan on.

The Chestertonians proposed a different approach. They said that instead of operating from the top down, we ought to take the human being, in his home, as the starting point and build a decentralized economy around him. They thought that people should own private property and the means to produce things—but not in obnoxious amounts, thus that *more* people might own private property and the means to produce things, thus that fewer people might live in poverty.

So you might say it is an economic model that favors the quadrant labeled *more privatized* and *more localized* as the most stable and resilient region of our economic systems graph. On the other hand, you might not say any such thing at all. Chesterton surely didn't—at least not that way. He and his ilk were not inclined to think of their idea as something that needed graphs, charts, textbooks, and systems analysts. It was, simply, the natural way to be a human going about your business, in all of its rich and earthy goodness.

It was the way that all healthy societies had operated in the past and the way all societies ought to start operating in the present. They didn't even seem that keen on giving the thing a name. But eventually, begrudgingly, it came to be called "distributism."

A core part of the concept is the belief that things ought to be produced as close to where they will be consumed as is efficaciously possible. For instance, if the only place to get your food is from another continent, you are in dehumanizing and dangerous territory. If you can get your food instead from mega-farms and enormous processing facilities a few hundred miles away, that may be tolerably better, but not by much—you're still relying on those operations operating, plus a network of middlemen and federal highways and refrigerated semi-trucks. If instead, you can get food from good farmers nearby, you should. It's a solid solution, and you might meet some people. And growing some of your own food, or maybe all of it, one hundred feet from where you'll eat it, is fantastic. Supply-chain disruptions and hyperinflation can't touch you, and the whole experience is rich and real, intimate and human. It happened to be exactly the way my wife and I wanted to do things, just because we wanted to do them exactly that way—even if it hadn't also happened to be a highly resilient and secure way.

And this brings us around to our baby daughter. She tipped us off to her distributist proclivities when she pushed the concept even further—proximity between production and consumption taken to its perfected end. My wife loved to hold her. My wife held our daughter while she slept in her arms, and she held our daughter when she woke and cooed and looked at the world, and in the most intimate and human of moments, when our baby daughter was hungry, my wife held her closer.

No matter how we came at it, with charts or "-isms" or books or babies, it always came around to the same thing. Distributism looked to be the way to live a beautiful, edifying human life *and* the way to build a stable, resilient economic society.

❖ ❖ ❖

All of this was an eye-opening and delightful surprise to us. It was a paradigm shift that went beyond the binary debate, turning the conversation inside out. But what were we missing? What were the downsides? We began reading literature that was critical of distributism to try to find out.

The gist of what we saw was the claim that distributism is simply unrealistic for a modern society. I wondered why. I knew that some of the most complex, modern, man-made systems in the world followed this same approach of intentional decentralization. Such systems never showed the cyclical boom and bust phenomenon that, for instance, the American economy perpetually exhibits. They were stable and resilient. And I always found it fascinating that we had learned to build such things by studying nature: real-world ecosystems, the human brain, all sorts of intricate wonders in Creation are distributed networks—a large number of small hubs of control spread about. So why was distributism unrealistic?

As far as I could tell, the claim rested on the shoulders of a strawman. People misportrayed distributism as some sort of implacable primitivism: "You can't have a modern society consisting only of subsistence farmers!" Agreed.

A guiding paradigm in distributism is called the *principle of subsidiarity*. The primitivism problem arose from a misunderstanding of this principle, thinking it simply endorses "localize!" as the answer to every possible question. Critics envision a return, I suppose, to near-universal agrarianism, an elimination of cars, airplanes, hospitals, modern militaries, and any industry that cannot be conducted in your neighborhood blacksmith shop. This is a misinterpretation, and it misses the point.

Right relation with the land and a healthy skepticism of dehumanizing technology are indeed key to the distributist worldview. And things local and small should be favored when that can work well. But by no means must everyone therefore be a subsistence farmer. The actual idea is much more nuanced. Properly stated, it is this: *Centralize what is best centralized; localize what is best localized; and when you can't tell which is best, localize.* The first two parts are obvious (but notice, dear aforementioned critics, the presence of the first). It is the third part that contains the subtle brilliance. This is the tie-breaker: what to do when we know not what to do. Modern capitalism and socialism centralize in the third scenario (and often the second). By instead localizing the gray zone, we distribute power safely; we avoid bottlenecks; we create a buffer in the system for times of crisis; we irrigate at the roots to promote balanced growth. We avoid all those problems I described that occur in complex systems with hyper-centralized architecture. Subsidiarity is the magic rule by which nature and all sustainable systems are built.

❖ ❖ ❖

It all made solid sense. The critics could be answered, and the whole thing seemed to offer a way of thinking and living that was both intelligent in design and intimate in disposition. Given all this, we had to wonder why it was not more widely practiced and why the centralization had occurred in the first place. How did we get here? And regardless, there remained this nagging question: can distributism be reconciled with Americanism?

In 1776, two pieces of writing that bear on these questions forever changed the course of human events. The one declared that

Localism

God gives people, among other things, the right to liberty. I think that is the heart of what draws traditionally minded Americans to capitalism. We cherish freedom. We are the land of liberty. We have a three-hundred-and-five-foot-tall statue to prove it. And in a curiosity of timing, in the same year the Founding Fathers made their Declaration defining America, the "Father of Capitalism," Adam Smith, published his defining work, *The Wealth of Nations*. Ever since, people seem to have been trying to merge the two documents. Capitalism promises liberty within the marketplace, and this resonates with everything we hold dear, everything Americans have bled and died to enshrine. A free market for a free people.

But in a fallen world, some of those free people can take the word "freedom" and begin to stretch it out of all recognizable shape. The American Revolution ended, but the Industrial Revolution carried on and grew, and with it grew the freedom of the market, until it began to eclipse other rights, including those actually listed in the Declaration. Any restrictions whatsoever on the market were now immoral, the new tyranny. And so with time, it became possible to think of a "good investment" as any profitable investment, regardless of whether it was good—regardless of the lives of employees, effects on communities, or degradation of Creation. Some people rose to immense wealth, borne on the weary backs of others and the depleting wealth of the planet.

Was this truly American? Our founders were suspicious of power being too tightly concentrated anywhere. We were thirteen loosely joined states—fervently maintaining all authority close to the people, except where it was clearly superior for the public good and common defense when held higher (a.k.a. the principle of subsidiarity). The economy was comprised of countless small businesses and farms; a great many people were landowners. There was disparity; "The poor you will always have with you." But understood for what it was, things were remarkably distributed, and this was understood to be a good thing, an American thing. It could equally well be called a distributist thing.

Or if we want, we could call it an early variety of capitalism, and probably a good one. Chesterton said, "Too much capitalism does not mean too many capitalists, but too few capitalists." We might even find our way around to our same appellation by speaking of "distributed capitalism": "distributism" for short; though doing so might rob us of a greater sphere of meaning, it would at least be a form of capitalism I could unambiguously get behind. But such capitalism had little resemblance to the hyper-centralized forms that came later. There was not an American in 1800 who, given the opportunity to meet a robber baron from 1900 or a hedge-fund manager from 2000 or a technocratic oligarch from today, would have exclaimed delightedly, "Ah, there is American capitalism at work!" In fact, no one in 1800 would have said "capitalism" at all. Despite the positive postmortem paternity test, Adam Smith never once used the word. The term was probably only beginning to see limited circulation in America around the time of the Civil War—just as (the winning) half of the nation was ardently asserting the belief that freedom of the market does not trump the freedom of men.

In pondering all this, we had to accept the fact that any American identification with unmitigated capitalism is a recent thing and a contrived thing, foisted on us by the unmitigated capitalists. Distributism not only reconciles with Americanism; distributism in a very real sense *is* Americanism (absent some individualism and Enlightenment corruption).

In socialism's history, my wife and I saw a movement also motivated by the desire for freedom—freedom from want, freedom from oppression—not of governments but of those very magnates who rose up within the freedom of markets. But, again, things go awry. The freedom from poverty shifts to freedom for the party—freedom to take control, reaching sometimes its communist extremes. It achieves its official aims in theories and manifestos, while achieving its power grabs in torturous reality.

In both cases, an expanding idea of freedom allows the power centers to freely expand. For the common man and society at large, this is dangerous and dehumanizing. But for the centralists, those elites at the center of the centralizing, it works out brilliantly. They are motivated to keep it going and to keep us from noticing that it's going.

Consider again our imaginary diagram. We tend to be fixated on the tug of war along that left-right axis. Pull to the left! Pull to the right! Our thoughts, debates, and campaign contributions are consumed back and forth on that line, in support of our preferred version of freedom. We really ought to be paying attention to the other line as well, the up-and-down one, navigating it with intentionality through subsidiarity. But as long as the centralists can keep us from doing so and keep everyone focused only on the left-right fight, which is never concluded, then they remain in power—be they bank owner or politburo.

Is this Americanism? That depends entirely on us. If America has ever meant anything good—and it has—this is not it. But in any case, it is the answer to the question of why we live out our twenty-first-century days under the curse of centralism.

❖   ❖   ❖

Such things were becoming clear as we were becoming parents. Reading distributists while rearing children gave shape and understanding to the natural, human longings we were feeling, the desire to rebel against the centralist lie. Everything that has happened since has only confirmed the sentiments. And the concerns about fragility have grown and, lately, greatly proven themselves. It is all as Chesterton said, except more so.

In these past years, with the Internet, global transit, and open trade, centralization has accelerated and amplified beyond imagination. A mere farm or factory is no longer the thing. The new capital asset of interest is the entire *network*, straddling the planet: website to warehouse, fabrication to fleet, digital assistant to delivery man, woman, or drone. It runs from the finance-capitalist West (consumption) to the socialist-communist East (production) and back again — an earth-sized infrastructure, a capital asset on which the sun never sets. And such a thing can be owned by a single, Amazonian-sized company. An elite race of Titan Technoligarchs has arisen. This is our economy today. Is it capitalism? Is it socialism? Yes, no, both — it is centralism.

And its fragility has now been put on spectacular display. A virus, one ten-millionth of a meter wide, jammed up the engines of the entire thing. Supply chains broke; medicine sources were in peril; food was destroyed en masse in agricultural areas as grocery store shelves sat empty. Add to it now social unrest, hyperinflation, and predictions of much wider American food shortages. While the virus is retreating, the cascade of ramifications seems to just be getting started. And coming through all of this, another child came to us (*Deo gratias*), our fifth: not all babies can be nourished in the same way she is, the same way her sister was, and that has been the case throughout history — but is it not a shocking cruelty to both mothers and children that the only other option offered by centralist society depends entirely on distant formula factories that have lately been closed?

We count ourselves fortunate. And we are all fortunate, those still here, to have survived a pandemic and all that has followed.

But we should not be surprised at what has followed. Centralized architectures only work well when everything goes as planned, and that hasn't been the case of late. We are surely blessed that their failures have not yet crushed us. But they ought to be a resounding wake-up call. It is time to change our ways. It is time to defund the plutocrats. Happily, their machine depends on us fulfilling our role as distant, addicted consumers. We are the pump that keeps it going. If we all opt out, if we stop, then it stops—replaced by something better, more secure, more beautiful. Right here, right where we are.

❖ ❖ ❖

Thirteen years have now passed since our first daughter was born. Her eyes have remained blue, her blonde hair is longer, and her distributist proclivities are in full bloom. Like her mother, she is drawn to gardens and kitchens and all beautifully productive places. Like her father at her age, she is drawn to matters mercantile: this week she is sewing a dress with pockets on the sides and buttons down the back for her first customer, half an hour south of us. It is the same with all of our children. We have tried not to push too hard; but indeed, the children often seem to be pulling us. Organically and of their own accord they come to these things. Distributism is inborn, a part of nature; capitalism and socialism are learned traits.

Our economic affiliation confusion feels now comfortably sorted. It was really all a matter of looking at things from a broader, truer perspective. As distributists are fond of saying, distributism is about more than just economics because economics is about more than just economics. In the end, it all comes together, and it all comes to this: If we were forced to choose between a rich life and a resilient society, we would at least have a decision to make.

But what a wonder that we do not! Providence would have us have both. The beauty of our human lives and the strength of our great land come of the same blessed things. The decision is simply what is the next right thing to *do* about it. Some people will do large things. Most will need to do small things, and small things are most of what's needed. Distributism requires no act of Congress. We the people hold all the power.

So I think we should just get started. Become a producer. Build up local economy. Plant a garden. Found a farm. Fix something instead of replacing it. Buy real things from real people. Start a business and sell real things to real people—focus on things real people actually need. Or maybe just start by canceling something you don't need; then cook dinner with your family to celebrate. When we do any of these things we add to the richness of our lives and move our communities and nation a small step toward resilience instead of vulnerability. Herein lies the liberty to truly be human. I think that is what they were talking about in the songs and on those monuments. That was the message sent across the dark oceans. Give me your huddled masses—not so that they might huddle again, under an identical oppressor with a different label, but that they might have something of their own, have work that is life-giving, a chance to be human, a chance to breathe free. If we can narrow our concept of freedom once again, we will expand it tremendously.

Go Back

Ryan Hanning

Moving back to the land will cure you of many things. First and foremost, it will cure you of any pride, self-dependence, or delusions of grandeur. This has been good news for me—when I am man enough to admit it. However, it was not what I intended. The idyllic landscapes, natural rhythms, increased family time, and promise of less artificial ecosystems, not to mention less artificial economics, attracted my wife and me to a more rural lifestyle. We wanted to lay in the peace of wild things "where the wood drake rests in his beauty on the water" not in the flickering amber hue of the streetlights of suburbia. Intellectually, I had prepared myself with a steady dose of Chesterton, Belloc, MacDonald, and more contemporary luminaries such as Aldo Leopold, and Wendell Berry.

Simultaneously, my wife dove deep into studying the practical and technical applications of various farming methodologies for growing crops, silviculture, mycology, and raising livestock. She made a trial run with these things in our small suburban backyard. This small-scale practice along with the intellectual formation was invaluable. However, certain things can only be learned by being. Like marriage, being in relationship with the land is a state of being, a habit of mind. Like a good marriage, being in right relationship with the land requires commitment, affection, and a good dose of dying to oneself. It also requires a lot of practical knowledge learned only through intimate, frequent failures and the guidance of trusted mentors. What follows here is not an apologetic for fleeing to the land but rather a confession of sorts of what we have learned and the practical considerations every would-be homesteader or farmer ought to consider.

One of my intellectual heroes once told me, "Nostalgia makes a poor excuse for tradition." No amount of running away from the abstractions of modernity will heal you of them. No amount of zeal overcomes your ignorance on its own. While nature is a great teacher, her powers are limited by our receptivity and docility to her lessons. Busyness, overconsumption, impatience, and the distractions of non-essential things are conditions of the Fall, not just city life. Unless you are willing to undergo a conversion of sorts, the sicknesses and abstractions of modernity will follow you onto the land, which has little pity for arrogant or stubborn pupils.

At its most basic, a person's homestead or farm is an ecological system you are in relationship with. Like all relationships, nothing replaces time and proximity. By time, I mean patience to learn the land: how and where the water flows, where the soils are richer and more conducive to growth, how the sun moves over the land throughout the seasons, what wildlife you are coexisting with. By proximity I mean time physically spent on the land: walking it, stewarding it, learning it, becoming aware of her specific idiosyncrasies. Chesterton and Belloc's vision of small homesteads was based on a plot of land capable for a man to know. Wendell Berry suggests never owning more land than you can walk in a day. Both time and proximity come only from working the land.

From preparing beds, planting, harvesting, and tending livestock. From an amazing amount of experimentation and failure.

Nature is an incredible teacher. The ways of nature are beautiful and wild. While they can be known to us, we rarely understand their complexity, and we are even more rarely willing to be guided by them. But enough philosophical opining. Suffice to say, anyone seeking to live closer to the land must be ready to receive the harshly beautiful lessons she provides. Here are some of the lessons we learned as we moved from the suburbs to our homestead.

Lesson 1: You cannot do it all at once.

The amount of time, knowledge, and physical ability to rightly live on the land takes longer than any YouTuber or Pinterest farmer admits. Most farmers have generations of technical knowledge customized to a specific location and well-honed muscles fit for the task, and most do it full-time. The fact that so many social media "homesteaders" make their living from their videos is an indication they have not yet figured out how to live on the land. We have learned we need to plan well and readily admit when we do not have the knowledge, physical ability, or the time. When missing knowledge, we consult mentors and books, or we hire contractors willing to teach us as they do the work. When lacking physical ability, we call in help or rent equipment. When time is scarce, we must make prudent adjustments to allot the time needed to focus on the priority.

At our homestead, we planned to grow enough food to feed our family (either directly or through trade). This calls for year-round crops and enough livestock to provide dairy and meat for our growing needs. Year-round crops require fields properly prepped, varieties of annuals and perennials suitable for our soil and climate, watering systems, amending of soil, sprouting and transplanting seedlings, sowing seeds, and harvesting. Livestock must be housed, fed, properly bred, raised to weight, and processed. We naively expected to do all this, have a surplus for trade, and get a reasonable amount of sleep, all while I continued to teach and work outside the home within the first year. We could not do it all at once. We needed more time to acquire knowledge, build infrastructure, and get expert help where needed.

We have learned a simple equation. Prudent discernment + careful planning + good execution = success 51 percent of the time. Planning for 49 percent failure may seem high, but when we build in enough buffer and expect a steep learning curve, we are able to learn and build from the lessons born of our failure without losing the homestead. In many areas we now have an 80 percent success rate!

It takes years to learn the land and build the infrastructure necessary to plant, grow, and harvest. Best to have an idea of what you want your homestead to be. Instead of making the common mistake of "we'll grow everything," humble oneself and consider what skills, desires, and infrastructure might already be there to start sensibly. Once you have sensible goals, gradually build up to them, starting with what you have the most knowledge, skills, and resources to achieve. As you fully immerse yourself in your homestead, you can begin to tackle the next steps, fine tuning them to better suit your location and family.

Lesson 2: Dirt is not soil.

I spend more time moving animal poop than any other single task on the homestead. This has come to me as quite a surprise, as it was never mentioned in any of the farming books of my childhood. I knew having livestock meant shoveling poop. However, I did not realize its volume or its value.

While some land is naturally rich and fertile, most is just abused dirt needing some amending to grow more crops than weeds. Dirt is not soil. Dirt is the medium in which soil is built. Unless dirt is fed nutrients, and without the microbiology necessary to unlock those nutrients, your plants will essentially starve. In one square foot of soil, there are hundreds of different types of organisms. It takes a long time for the organisms to create a thriving ecosystem that makes up soil. Fertilizers are well and good and can provide quick nutrients directly to the plant, but they are not a long-term strategy to improve soil quality and fertility. If you do not want to till in massive amounts of chemicals—much of which is not available nor cost effective for the homesteader or small farmer—then you will need to find other sources of improving soil fertility, and lots of it.

Good soil is alive, and like any living thing it needs discerning stewardship and management. Most of our soil is made by adding layers of animal manure, composted food, and old leaves to the dirt in contoured beds. Rabbit and goat manure are essentially pelletized nitrogen bombs we place directly into the beds. Cow and chicken manure—still too hot (very high in nitrogen) to put on the plants directly—are raked into piles to compost and age until being delivered to the field along with composted horse manure from a stall up the road. Like shampoo instructions, you do this once and then repeat. Forever.

Lesson 3: Raising livestock requires a different type of calculus.

The first rule of raising livestock is to make sure you know not only what your animals need but also the simple math to see if the potential output (meat, milk, eggs, etc.) justifies your input (time, money, stress, etc.). Different types of livestock require very different levels of care and skill. Raising chickens—the gateway drug of livestock—is pretty idiot-proof once you have built the right infrastructure; goats and cows, on the other hand, require daily care and tie you to the home.

Laying hens need water, food, and shelter from weather and predators. You do not need an elaborate set-up, but some thought ought to be given to each of these things: a bucket for water, a feeder for supplemental feed, a coop for shelter at night, a light for the winter months (hens need around fourteen to sixteen hours of light to lay). Add a rooster, an incubator, and a few extra hours seasonally to hatch chicks, and you are quickly moving toward a sustainable set-up. Raising the chicks to laying age (about sixteen to twenty-four weeks depending on breed) and keeping them fed and safe from predators ends up costing us about $1.50 per dozen. If you raise the larger breeds of laying hens, you can regularly cull the older hens for your dinner table, adding further value to raising chickens. At first, processing the poultry will be a bit arduous and will take a considerable amount of time. But similar to the increasing returns of keeping hens, the more you butcher, the better and more efficient you will become. Soon an investment of an hour or two will give you three to five pounds of fresh meat per chicken.

Rabbits raised for meat provide even better output to input ratios, providing more meat and incredible pelts to be tanned and sold. Again, building the infrastructure and learning the skills make the economics unfavorable at first, but soon the increasing returns make economic sense. Another reason for carefully developing sustainable infrastructure: as you improve efficiencies in your production, the costs continue to come down. We estimate our rabbit meat that we self-process ends up costing us about $2 per pound, not including any costs offset by selling the pelts.

Goats raised for milk require some additional gear, even if you are milking them by hand. They need plenty of fresh food, water, and frequent rotation to prevent high parasite load, which robs them of nutrients and makes them sick. While goats may chew just about anything, they are actually really picky in what they will eat. They are browsers, not grazers, and they need a lot of attention. They also need specialized fencing to prevent them from constantly escaping. Our goats are milked each morning and evening, and we estimate that we have gotten our costs down to about a $1 per gallon.

Beef requires more infrastructure in fencing, watering, pasturing, breeding, and transporting. It also requires more knowledge for handling, breeding, and processing. We prefer the Chestertonian vision of a small cattle operation. We maintain a milk cow and a meat cow that we send to a butcher for the final processing. The increased costs make beef a little less economically viable. Our first bull cost us about $4 per pound. Not too bad for organic, grass-fed beef, but not enough margin to make a significant profit if we were to sell beef.

Honestly, managing the livestock requires considerable physical and mental energy. It is highly dependent on your region and what breeds you raise. Learning to move our cows safely and effectively and daily herding our sheep into paddocks has been a steep learning curve. If you included hours spent in learning these skills and daily caring for the animals, the economic reality does not make a lot of sense. One is tempted to compare the hours spent with what they would have made as a wage earner. Often, I think to myself, how much meat could I buy with one hour of work outside the home. This consideration ought to be examined. Cold, hard calculations show homesteading is often much less efficient than large-scale commercial operations. Big commercial outfits run at a scale that provides efficiencies most small-scale farms cannot compete with. However, raising livestock requires a different economic calculus. It must be examined in light of the whole picture of the gains received. Hours on the field with the family, mornings and evenings with the kids milking goats. Friendships formed with those you learn to depend on for purchasing, processing, or moving your livestock. The satisfaction of being able to provide someone with meat raised on your land. Not to mention the mental stamina and virtues gained by the constant failures and setbacks.

Lesson 4: Becoming a member requires commitment.

All places are made up of communities, and all communities are made up of members. We do not often think of this in our placeless society where our commitments to people and place are usually only constrained by economic considerations. However, in more rural communities, the sense of place and local culture is very real. One can live in a community without ever being a member. That is, without ever joining the community.

In our little slice of existence, the community is strong, and becoming a member is not announced at a town hall and affirmed by a handshake from the mayor. We do not have a town hall, and the closest thing we have to a mayor is Mr. Brown, a retired cop whose family makes up most of the legendary stories in our region. Membership is less formal, but real, nonetheless. It requires that you demonstrate a commitment to the people and place. Practically, it means I buy sweet potatoes at the local grocery store even though they are more expensive because I know they came from Eric's farm and Eric has a growing family, not to mention he provides the hops for the local beer I like. I would not want Eric, his family, or his hops to leave our community. It means I ask my neighbor for a recommendation on who I should hire to fix my septic because chances are she knows someone local who cares if flushing my toilet might pollute the creek.

This is not a description of Mayberry; this is just common-sense, and it is how most of the world actually works. The more removed from the people and sources of production, the more abstracted our interaction is, which reduces our culpability and affability toward our neighbor. St. Thomas listed affability under the heading of justice. It is a matter of justice to give others what they are due. I ought to have a higher sense of commitment to my community, my people and place; after all, my existence and theirs depend on one another. Simply put, humans behave better when they are in relationship with the people and resources they depend on. One of the deepest lessons I have learned by living on the land is that distributism makes not only an economic claim but an anthropological one as well. A claim that we are dependent in large degree on each other and ought to act like it.

Lesson 5: Find your niche (i.e., lead with what you're good at).

Some things come easier than others on the homestead. Sometimes the land is more docile to your stewardship. Sometimes you are more docile to the land's counsel. Whichever is the case, you will inevitably find certain things work better than others. These are the things that you ought to focus on. We are good at raising goats for producing high-quality milk and subsequently cheese. We do many other things for good reason, but if we wanted to move into an operation that provided an income stream, this would be the likely choice. We are also good at raising peppers, but not on a scale that would compete with other growers. We are successful in growing hemp, but the market is complex, and processing it is very labor intensive.

Localism

It sounds elementary, but if you seek to produce a meaning-ful income from the land, you have to find your niche. Finding something you are good at is hard enough, but finding a market that will pay you what your time is worth is even harder. But even if it doesn't go far in the market, finding a focus still has its benefits and provides something that can be tended and improved over time, like the homestead itself. This is where lesson four (above) comes in. Being a member of your community helps develop the knowledge and support necessary to create products that serve the local common good as well as provide a profit.

Moving back to the land was a stupid decision from every mod-ern metric of economic value. My homestead demands long hours, does not have a 401K or stock options, and does not provide sick leave. However, it was the best bad decision we have made. We are paradoxically more secure (less dependent on the abstractions of modernity and market fluctuations) and yet more dependent on God and others than ever before. Living on the land is not for the prideful or faint of heart, and if you happen to suffer from either of those vices, the land will gladly cure you of them.

An African's Encounter with G. K. Chesterton

JOHN KANU

As a child in Kabonka, a small village in northern Sierra Leone, I experienced first-hand how African communitarian values are in tandem with G. K. Chesterton's distributist ideas. In addition to social and resource justice that can be derived from the practice of distributism in poor agrarian communities, we have seen through our work in the Sierra Leone Chesterton Society (SLCC) that the idea of distributism can not only be applied but that it builds local people's capacity to gain self-confidence and be free from the shackles of economic and social bondage.

In my village, unlike many other places today, every family and, by extension, everyone was very happy and contented. People were happy and contented because every family had fair access to the village resources: land and the natural spring well on which every household depended for their drinking water. These were the days when there was no television (still the case today, to a large extent) to ominously tell the village community about the terrible things happening in the outside world. There was not even a radio to inform the villagers about what was going on, such as which football team had won or who was now governing the country. There were no problems about plumbing or the hassle of paying electricity bills because up to this day, there is no electricity or supply of pipe-born water. In fact, at the time of my birth in 1964, my village was only connected to the outside world through a bush path that led to the next village and then several other villages until eventually you bumped up to Makeni, the district headquarters town of northern Sierra Leone. People from my village would have to trek on foot a round-trip distance of twenty-five miles to access basic modern health and education services in Makeni. Although a car can now reach my village, there was, thankfully, very little the community lacked or couldn't do without in 1964.

People of my village were happy and contented because the village's simple and transparent governance system ensured the physical and social protection of the village community. That allowed peace to reign so that the peasant population would be able to farm uninterrupted. Above all, there was and still is today, to some extent, love and concern for every member of the village. In those days, the needs of any member of our community were the needs of the whole village. Many times I witnessed how all members of the village came together and pooled their individual resources to solve the needs of the whole village without outside or donor assistance. Every household would contribute some cereals or vegetables to make sure that the food needs of a bereaved family and the poor village widow were met. The young men and women—the key providers of labor—would work for free on the rice fields of the old or childless households. Child-minding and moral discipline were not only the obligation of the parent but also the responsibility of every adult in the village.

In front of every mud hut was a small patch of a garden growing fine crops and vegetables—a few tomatoes, cucumbers, peppers, cassava, onions, and even plants for remedial medicine to treat the most common diseases. The forests were lush, serene, and full of good things. There were mango and orange trees, bananas and other exotic fruit plants at the backyards that provided important nutrients for the village community but also served as "circuses" where the children, especially the boys, spent a good numbers of hours per week in the dry seasons in climbing contests. Similarly, the tropical rivers were clean, and women and the young girls spent a similar number of hours per week in the long, dry seasons in artisanal freshwater fishing. In addition to the domestic gardens, once a year, each household would cultivate an average of two acres of rice mixed with other cereals—just enough to feed all the members of the household and, perhaps, ensure a little leftover for the stranger, a passerby, or those who were vulnerable or may be struggling to have enough food because of a poor harvest.

I remember vividly the joy and vibrancy that exuded in the village when the plants were ready and the harvest season had arrived. The children were at liberty to help themselves to huge quantities of mangoes or other fruits, irrespective of whose garden or farm they visited. Every household had a few chickens and some ruminants—goats and sheep. There was the village blacksmith whose training was in the first place supported by the village, and upon acquiring such skills, he would manufacture or tend to all the agricultural tools needed to support the village agrarian economy with no recourse to pecuniary payments.

There was also Pa Momoh Sesay, the wise and uncorrupted village chief who adjudicated over the village palavers with a strong sense of fairness and justice. Unlike the top-down dictatorships we see today, Pa Momoh would only intervene when such palavers could not be handled by the clan or family head. The village medicine man or woman who treated the more serious illnesses was very revered, and so was the town Cryer who disseminated messages or summoned a meeting at the village square, where all members of the community would give their opinion on matters that related to the welfare and well-being of the village. The village drummer, the dancer, the wrestler, and a celebrated storyteller were all the social capital the village possessed, and each played key roles in socializing and enriching life in an unadulterated African village. The net outcome was that everyone was well fed and very contented, lived in perfect harmony with their environment and their neighbors, and of course, felt at peace with their God.

Unfortunately, we are about to lose these beautiful and gospel-truth ways of life and ideals. Instead, the modern world at the behest of its scientific and startling technological discoveries appears more attuned toward a life that is getting more and more comfortable. The cost of our incrementally comfortable lives, however, outweighs the advantages. We are now confronted with an uncaring world order, a world that is marred in a ruthless agenda to devour and plunder everything on its way in the name of making life easy. Sadly, only few receive and enjoy the comfortability of the modern world to the detriment of the majority.

Today, the impact of this ruthless agenda is felt everywhere, even in my village, either in the form of extensive environmental degradation caused by reckless mineral exploitation by powerful multinational mining companies or food insecurity affecting millions of smallholder farmers throughout West Africa as a result of incremental effects of climate change. At the national level, the government is unwilling or incapable, relying heavily on multilateral borrowing from the World Bank or the International Monetary Fund (IMF) to provide basic services. Non-Government Organizations (NGOs) came a decade ago to "rescue" what was left of Sierra Leone at the end of one of Africa's most brutal wars in 2002. While the contribution of NGOs undeniably did some good and saved some lives, their impact would have been greater if they had aligned their support according to the culture, aspirations, and priorities of the people—not the top-down development model in which village people were told that their lives were miserable and that all the food aid supplies and the new things provided by the NGOs would make them live productive and civilized lives. It was clear from this point that the people from my village can no longer afford to be so contented. No wonder that even in those days, the elders of our village often talked about the need for the younger generation to learn how to read and write. They discussed the need to have health care and a proper road to the big town of Makeni.

My life started getting complicated at age eight when I tormented my father and his household to get me registered in a local school in the next village. Several meetings were held by my family household. Some, rightly so, were skeptical about sending me to school. They were concerned about who would inherit the farm and our traditions. Others were of the view that the new world was the future, and therefore it was important to have the younger generation learn how to read and write. The matter was adjourned until my mother's clan in a nearby village had their say. Fortunately, it didn't take long: the decision from my mother's side came in favor that I should be sent to school. At least that would make me stop tormenting the fruit trees. I suspected my mother's mother, who was fond of calling me her "husband," had a hand in this decision.

Now, although October 6, 1964, is quoted in all my official documents as the date I was born, I am not really sure of this date at all. My parents and all the members of my village community were illiterate, and there was no formal system like a clinic or school to register my birth. In those days, knowledge of or lack of one's date of birth was irrelevant in almost all parts of rural Sierra Leone. In fact, one's age was judged by your height and looks. Forget about the precise time of day, date, and month you were born because no one had or knew how to read a watch or a calendar in the village. Instead, the commonest way to mark one's year of birth was tied to the living calendar of the village itself. For example, a parent will tell your age either by the year a particular plot of land was farmed by the household or by an important event that occurred in the year you were born.

So there I was in September 1972, waiting in line to be registered in a local school in the next village three-and-a-half miles away from my village. To stand before your headmaster to answer questions regarding your biodata on the first day in school was a terrifying experience. Why was the headmaster asking every child for his or her date of birth? What benefit would he possibly get from such information?

These were the questions and emotions going on in my head until it was my turn. I had no clue what to say other than the fact that I was so nervous and feared that I would be turned away from school for being so ignorant about something so straightforward as my date of birth. I guess the other children must have felt the same because the headmaster was left empty handed by the end of the first school day. We were ordered to find out from our parents and make sure the information was available the next school day. No doubt, finding out about our dates of birth was our first major bit of homework.

Back to my village that evening, I gave my father no respite after a day's work in the fields. Straight away, I bombarded him with questions about the day, time, month, and year of my birth. The poor man had no clue about these things. From the vestiges of his mental library, this is what he said to me: "You were born the year they changed the national currency from the British pound sterling to the present Sierra Leone Leones (SLL)." Paltry though this was, I took the data to school the following day, and that seemed to have satisfied the headmaster because there were no further questions, and for the time being, my registration was completed. Many years later, when I was in a position to visit a library and read and comprehend basic texts, I discovered that the change of currency from the British pound sterling to the Sierra Leone Leones occurred sometime in 1964, and so I adopted that year as my year of birth. But as you can see, the issue of my date of birth had still not been fully resolved and lingered on until a much later date during yet another encounter that I will narrate later.

I completed my secondary education in 1985 with fairly good grades to go to the local university. Alas! I couldn't go to university straight away because my family couldn't afford the tuition fee, which was, at the time, the equivalent of roughly $32 per annum. You have to be highly connected with people in the national government to gain a scholarship to the local university. People from my village didn't have that luxury. I said to myself, *What next?* To have stayed in the village after wasting all those years with only a fifth-form education would have been devastating.

I was caught on a pendulum of a vicious dilemma: I had lost the prime time of my youth, when I could have had the "education" of my Limba tribe, acquiring the tribe's major livelihood skills such as palm-wine tapping, farming, and hunting, instead of a western education that at the fifth form did not go far. Perhaps the best thing my fifth-form education would do was facilitate communication between members of my family with their distant relatives through letter writing. Like most young people today, I was forced with a stab in my heart to leave my beautiful village for the uncertainty of life in Freetown, the capital, in search of opportunity.

I was lucky in many ways because after a year of relentless search and a cocktail of menial jobs, I ran into Canon Fr. Herbert Victor

Veal, the then only and very compassionate English Catholic priest. Canon Veal's commitment and the yard stick that defined his life and work in Sierra Leone was "option for the poor." After Mass one Sunday in 1987, I approached him and confronted him with my "education dilemma" and how desperately I wanted to continue my education and fulfil the dream of my family, especially those who voted that I should be "educated."

On that day I will never forget, this disciple of God said to me, "My boy, don't you in your predicament think that God has forgotten about you. Never be tempted to think that your problem is the end of the world. In fact, anything that diminishes you makes you great.... I can't promise you anything. Let us pray together about this."

His eyes were so serene and pure and his soft and gentle voice so soothing that I was convinced of his sincerity when I left his presbytery office. That conversation did a lot of good to my soul and has stayed with me to this day. He had asked me to visit him three days a week to help him dispatch letters to his parishioners, and on many occasions, I accompanied him in visiting the sick at the Connaught hospital or the dying in their homes. He was a man of deep Christian faith and remarkable compassion. From the misery he saw every day, he asked me to form a local lay fraternity of volunteers to provide care to a new and alarming problem: "street children." These street children were the earliest signs of a Sierra Leonean society that was at the brink of total dysfunctionality, as witnessed by the events that unfolded a few years later.

Apart from being a very pious and compassionate man, this English priest was also a man with a keen sense of humor. He frequently invited us, the fraternity volunteers, to prayer retreats followed by splendid lunches or dinners. It was during one of those dinners in 1989, after two years that we had known each other and were working together, when the problem of my date of birth was finally resolved. Over a pint of beer and having fun, he suddenly asked, "John, what's your date of birth and how old are you now?"

I was completely taken aback, given the occasion, and as I never expected the question, I stammered, "Maybe twenty-five, Father, but I can't tell you my exact date of birth."

Surprised and thoroughly amused, he said, "But how come?" I responded that it was because my parents were illiterate and I was born in the village and my birth was never registered. He said, "My mother was born on October 6 in England, the Feast of St. Bruno. Why can't you consider that to be your birthday?" Done! This man of God will never know the weight he lifted off my shoulders. At last, here was one person to validate my birth date. From that day on, October 6 has been my date of birth, and let us hope that it providentially coincides with the actual date I was born. From there on also and through his help, I was able to combine work with a spell in the local university, and I am one of the first products locally trained in social work and community development. This was the highest possible education one could get in the social sciences in Sierra Leone, but it was hardly enough to quench my thirst for learning.

As if by divine providence, one encounter led to another encounter. Three years into my studies, Fr. Veal facilitated the invitation of the Mill Hill–based Daughters of Charity of St. Vincent de Paul from London to open a charity in Freetown called the House of Light for street girls. I became the charity's first and leading community worker and, together with the sisters, we brought some respite to many families in the slums of Freetown. However, this good work was not meant to last, as the sisters were forced to flee following the first rebel attack on Freetown in November 1994. I was once again jobless and back on the streets looking for a job or, what I hoped, a place in a university to improve my level of knowledge and skills.

It was while working with the sisters, however, that one of them, the noble-hearted Sr. Patricia Maxwell, saw in me the restless passion to continue my education. Sr. Patricia knew of Plater College in Oxford, and because I was already past thirty years and father to my first son, Charles, the sister thought Plater College would be an excellent opportunity for my educational needs. The story of how I got to Oxford is perhaps what Chesterton would have described as "a bold attempt in turning folly into reality." In my wildest dreams, there was no way I could afford the cost of going to Oxford—a fact my friends and family constantly kept reminding about. But there was a bigger problem beyond cost. Due to the protracted nature of the war marred by high levels of human-rights abuses (indiscriminate killings, rape, and limb hacking), Sierra Leone was placed under a U.N.-sponsored arms embargo that banned all flights or ships from visiting Sierra Leone. The consular section of the British Embassy in Freetown was not functioning because the British High Commissioner, Mr. Peter Penfold, was embroiled in the Sandline scandal.

So I could not obtain a visa from Sierra Leone to go to Oxford even if I had the money to defray the cost of travel. The preferred alternative for Sierra Leoneans to obtain a visa would be a visit to The Gambia and, from there, proceed to the U.K. Besides, all of Sierra Leone, with the exception of Freetown, was under rebel control at the behest of international criminal cartels plundering the country's diamonds and other natural resources. The perception of the outside world about Sierra Leone was that of a failed state, a country so marred in corruption and barbarity that it could not be saved. It was inherently disposed to doom. This was not an ideal moment to seek help for academic pursuits.

These obstacles notwithstanding, I set about exploring ways to get to Oxford. Each year from 1995 to 1999, I would post an application letter for a scholarship to the principal of Plater College. I suspect that the principal, Mr. Michael Blades (whom I later came to admire very deeply), and his team got so fed up with my application letters (as Fr. Veal would have said, "get the wolf off your door") that they finally decided to offer me the Colt Foundation scholarship in 1999. Of course, there were some conditions attached: I would have to buy a round-trip ticket to and from the U.K., and I should return to Sierra Leone immediately after my year at Plater College.

They needn't have to worry about the second condition (my return to Sierra Leone after my studies). About the first, Fr. Veal berated the college administration, "How dare you expect a student from a burning country to pay for his passage to the U.K.?" At any rate, it seemed that the obstacles to get me to the U.K. would never end because in 1999, Sierra Leone was burning, and my house, the most valuable possession I had apart from my miserable life and family, had just been burned down by the rebels a couple of months before.

Where on earth would I ever get $400 for the ticket? I sold the remains of my house (not the land), such as the steel doors and windows, and for the rest, I turned to members of my family for help. The family, as always, serves as our bank and welfare state. No financial institution would provide me with a loan. There was no sitting government to ask for help. Between the sale of my house items and donations from family and friends, we raised $450. I set off for The Gambia in September 1999, and through the intervention of the British High Commissioner's wife, the venerable Celia Penfold, I got the visa to the U.K. Guess who was my first host in the U.K.? Fr. Veal, who had retired to the U.K. I stayed a couple of days in East London with my old friend and mentor.

Localism

On October 4, 1999, I took the X-90 coach to Oxford. There I met a soft-spoken English man who would have a life-changing impact on me. He was a God-sent lecturer, and his name was Stratford Caldecott (of blessed memory). Dr. Caldecott was the master of the Christianity and Society (C&S) class at Plater College, a Catholic residential college founded in 1921 in Oxford in memory of Fr. Charles Plater, SJ, to provide a second-chance education opportunity for Catholic workers who, like me, had dropped out of mainstream education because they had to find work to fend for their families. It was from Caldecott through his soul-reaching tutorials in his small office room at Plater College that I learned about G. K. Chesterton and his ideas of distributism.

What was it that so much fascinated me about G. K. Chesterton, an Englishman who never came to Africa? I was struck by his candor and the parallels in his writings to my experiences of community life in Africa. In other words, Chesterton in his distributist writings gave expression to the best qualities of traditional African communitarian values. Although I left with a master's degree in the social sciences from Oxford University, attending Stratford's C&S classes was the best education experience I got from Oxford. My providential encounter with Stratford Caldecott set off a litany of other encounters. The truth is, there is no way I could have returned to Sierra Leone after three years living in Oxford with my family if I had not met Stratford and discovered Chesterton. This encounter fulfilled the dream and the commitment I made to my village folks to have one of their own "educated."

Today, two little initiatives are taking hold in Sierra Leone in honor and fulfilment of G. K. Chesterton's ideas: the Sierra Leone Chesterton Center (SLCC) and our Chesterton Academy.

The SLCC was founded in Sierra Leone in 2006 as a community-based organization (CBO). The SLCC goal is to respond to the growing concentration of wealth in the country's elite class of a few powerful people and to offer a different development approach that is centered on cooperative formation and capacity building in rural communities like my village. It is important to reorient local people's capacity to maintain and retain the positive qualities of African communitarian values that have dignified rural life with parallels to Chesterton's distributist ideas. In the end, we want to revitalize rural communities with greater access to resources and the means of production by as many members of local communities as possible.

Unlike other development models, our work is realized by building existing community social infrastructures and using such structures and cultural platforms such as storytelling and drama to galvanize community action to improve food security and enhance community access to critical services. For example, rather than imposing our lofty ideas, we would, at the end of a day's work in the rice fields, sit with the villagers around a gentle fire trough or under a mango tree's shade and tell stories that provoke critical thinking among the villagers related to their needs. From there, we would facilitate a process in which the villagers themselves would identify what strengths and resources they have to resolve their needs with little or without outside funds.

It is only after absolutely exhausting the identification of existing local resources that we would bring in supplies like nails, zinc for the health center, or cement for the construction of the village school. Our supplies, in many cases, involve nothing more than training on agronomy or environmental-friendly farming techniques.

Importantly, we spend significant efforts and time on mediation between chiefs and mining companies whose investments trample on the land needs of smallholder farmers. Rather than acting as the *vox populi*, however, we organize smallholder farmers into cooperatives and train them in advocacy and negotiation skills to better resist their land competitors and thus sustain their right to food in their localities. SLCC's focus to protect land is not misplaced because land, in traditional Africa values, is not just a place to grow crops for food but also a resource with aesthetic cultural, social, and spiritual values.

To start with, land does not belong to one person but to the whole family or clan. It is a resource to be tended with care and honest stewardship and to be passed on from one generation to the other. Land symbolizes the connection between the past and the present. It is on this same land that our ancestors had toiled and taken responsibility for their community and offspring, and, therefore, the next generation should be desirous to do the same.

It is interesting to mention at this point that our little contribution working with chiefs on land issues resulted to an important outcome. Just a short while ago, there was an outcry from the country's traditional leaders resisting the new Land Rights Bill introduced by the central government. If this bill is passed into law, it will allow unfettered investment in agriculture by large-scale agribusinesses to the detriment of smallholder farmers, who represent 58 percent of the population dependent on agriculture. The chiefs' message to the national government was clear when they said, "Land in rural Sierra Leone is not for sale," that it is a resource to be used fairly and must be accessible to all members of village communities. That is exactly what the SLCC has been working on and will continue to work on. And so the SLCC does not consider itself an NGO, since NGOs come and go or shut down when donor funds run out. The SLCC, however, is part of the community, and we will stay as long as it is necessary.

The first pillar of SLCC's work is *cooperative formation*: we assist poor people in their daily efforts to feed their families. Rather than bring in food supplies, we help smallholder farmers to organize into farmer cooperatives and train them to increase their yields. The process is informal and is openly conducted under a tree or a shed. Community members discuss and are made to understand the problems that affect their livelihoods (land access, water, social and environmental issues, lack of appropriate agronomic skills, etc.) and agree on a number of community-based actions to resolve these problems. To date, more than three thousand smallholder farmers have participated in this program, yielding great outcomes, including improvement in crop production and better incomes.

The second pillar is *capacity building.* During the last four years, the SLCC introduced the production of improved maize and provided training to hundreds of smallholder farmers in Kono. Maize is not the staple food crop of Sierra Leone, so no wonder that our cooperative farmers were somewhat hesitant to grow maize. Both the SLCC and the initial trainees underestimated the income generation potential of maize. We were horrified that we may have introduced something "foreign and unneeded" and risked becoming another NGO. Then I took a market survey to find out who was out there that would buy maize from our cooperative farmers, and that is how I stumbled on to Fr. Joseph Turay, the vice chancellor of the University of Makeni and co-owner of one of the biggest poultries in the country. It was while I was sharing my fears with Fr. Joe (as he is popularly known) that he said, "We have just imported a forty-foot container of maize from Italy for our poultry at the cost of $20,000."

I couldn't believe my ears, so I said, "Why don't we make a pact that you buy from our farmers rather than importing from Italy?" Fr. Joe agreed!

Meanwhile, in a development meeting in Freetown, I learned that the United Nations Food and Agricultural Organization

(UNFAO) was going around establishing poultries all over the country as part of its Small and Medium Enterprises (SME) and youth empowerment program and that sixteen such SMEs were being established in Kono. What a God-sent opportunity! Today we have an active Memorandum of Understanding for SLCC farmers to provide maize to some of these SMEs, contributing greatly to the incomes of hundreds of smallholder farmers in Kono and allowing children from these families to attend the university.

The Chesterton Academy of Sierra Leone is the first educational initiative in Africa dedicated to popularize G. K. Chesterton's ideas of distributism. The school will give preference to children from disadvantaged communities in Sierra Leone. We aim to build local capacity in science and technology in the tradition of Catholic Social Teaching and faith, accompanied by fun in the spirit of G. K. C. The school's motto is a quotation by Chesterton, "Science is either a tool or toy," which was kindly sourced by the indefatigable servant Dale Ahlquist. From this school, we hope to scale up to a Chesterton College in the future where a new generation of doctors, nurses, and leaders would be trained to address the extensive health and poverty challenges facing our communities with compassion.

Dwelling Beside

My parish is finalizing the capital campaign that supported our recent church expansion project. Early phases of the project moved the church's meeting space from the basement to a new addition at ground level. Along with space to gather outside of Mass, the new addition includes offices, kitchen space, and other modern amenities designed to facilitate fellowship. I feel like I understand why we undertook this project, but I'm not proud of what we did.

As poor and isolated Catholics in a remote part of Minnesota, my great-grandparents and their peers a century ago managed to build a gorgeous cathedral to worship the Lord, one that will stand until we allow it to fall. With our far greater resources and capacity, we managed to construct an addition that, were it not appended to the church and partially clad in stone veneer, would be right at home in any standard office park. It may be functional, but its presence doesn't glorify that which our ancestors bequeathed to us.

I don't question the intentions of our leadership, but it is difficult not to witness this alteration as part of a broader change of emphasis, one that reflects society's shift to value the expedient over the enduring. Looked at today, the approach used to construct the original church—both the physical construction and the community that supported it—seems unfathomable, even ludicrous. As Catholics, we seem to want to stand apart, but not too far apart, from the broader culture we inhabit.

Nowhere is this more on display than in the rear of the present church, which has now been transformed into the new entrance. It's not that the old front lacked a great entrance; it had a beautiful pitched roof with carvings, stained glass, and a statue of St. Francis, our namesake. The old front entrance was a magnificent and humbling path to approach worship, but it lacked the most important feature for a twenty-first century Catholic church in America: convenient parking.

The old back is now the new front, and it has lots of parking. The statue of St. Francis no longer sits next to the steps that lead to the nave. Now it now sits on the opposite side of the building, at the end of the new parking lot, next to a dumpster. I live in the neighborhood and walk by this scene nearly every day. It makes me profoundly sad.

The new parking lot is the third we have created adjacent to the church. We accomplish this act of deconstruction by pooling our resources to purchase and then remove homes that used to make up the neighborhood. Where early Christians came together to live in common, we have an active program of dispersal, denuding the neighborhood the church sits within while facilitating the scattering of our parishioners.

As I write, we have plans to tear down additional buildings to add even more parking. In that, the community of St. Francis Parish has aligned itself with American society's passion for isolated living and commuter culture. Our parish has many urgent needs, but there seems to be no satiating our desire for more and more parking spaces.

The story of my community is deeply personal to me, but it's not an isolated example. I've had the opportunity to travel around the United States and visit both Catholic and Protestant parishes. It's clear we are all struggling with the same pressure to subordinate our practices to fit into modern American culture. In the larger picture, parking lots can seem like the least of our compromises.

We lost the parish. It profoundly damages us.

The English word "parish" descends from the Greek *paroikia*, a combination of *para* ("beside, subsidiary") and *oikos* ("dwelling"). We think of a parish as a community of people that attend a specific church, but it actually denotes the combination of both a people and a place. The parish was the community whose lives were spent together in physical and spiritual closeness to the church.

The reason for this closeness is obvious, but I'll state it here anyway: we are broken people, sinners in what we have done and what we have failed to do. As Catholics, the redemption we seek comes through a closeness to God, both a physical presence we experience in worship and a spiritual presence we witness in fellowship with others. We need *both* people and place. There is little about the Catholic faith that thrives in isolation from others.

I count myself foremost among those in need of redemption. I struggle day to day with living my faith as fully as I'm called to do. My lowest moments coincide with the times in my life when practicing Catholicism means a weekly obligation to be pursued with as minimal inconvenience as possible, when my fellow Catholics are people I smile at in the pews and the parking lot, not people I walk hand in hand with, pursuing life on Earth as it is in Heaven.

To be the best version of myself, I need my fellow Catholics. I need to worship with them. I need to practice our faith along with them. I need to walk through life with them. I don't believe I'm alone in this.

Localism

During Mass, we share with each other the sign of peace just prior to asking the Lamb of God to grant us peace. These are not greetings of friendship or expressions of frivolity; they are a sober expression of solidarity. Together, we are undertaking the most solemn part of our worship, supporting each other, at peace with God.

That support need not end at the conclusion of Mass, when we depart in our automobiles until we meet again next week. That experience is very modern and uniquely American. Such a casual relationship to each other would be unfathomable to my grandparents and their peers, let alone the many generations of Catholics that came before them.

Yet the pandemic provided a preview of the future of a Church that embraces and facilitates the denuding of its parish, the physical separation of a people from a place. Like millions of other Catholics, I experienced worship through the internet for the many months my church was shuttered. It was startlingly easy to fulfill my weekly obligation in my pajamas, on the couch, just a remote control click between the final prayer and the opening kickoff. If church attendance is reduced to being a function of convenience, there are more ways for us to degrade our worship once we finally have the church fully surrounded by asphalt pavement and halogen lights.

As G. K. Chesterton writes in *Orthodoxy*, "When a religious scheme is shattered, it is not merely the vices that are let loose. The vices are, indeed, let loose, and they wander and do damage. But the virtues are let loose also; and the virtues wander more wildly, and the virtues do more terrible damage." With the best of intentions, we have shattered the meaning of "parish"—the combination of a people and a place—and now, in many ways, we are, as Chesterton states, "isolated from each other and are wandering alone."

Humans don't thrive in isolation. We don't do well wandering alone. This is true of Catholics, but it is also true in the larger secular world, as we see all too clearly. We have an epidemic of loneliness in America, with one in three suffering from "serious loneliness." For young adults, it is 61 percent. For mothers of young children, it is 51 percent. How can any Christian—especially those who value life—not find those statistics staggering and in need of an urgent response?

Depression is endemic in America. Major depressive disorders affect approximately 17.3 million American adults, or about 7.1 percent of the U.S. population age eighteen and older, in a given year. The sick and the elderly suffer at far higher rates. The suicide rate has climbed for the past two decades. Suicide is the tenth leading cause of death for all Americans, the second leading cause for those under thirty-five. (Ironically, the leading cause of death for those under thirty-five is accidents, primarily automobile crashes.)

Abortion. Out of wedlock births. Divorce. Spousal abuse. Drug and alcohol addiction. Obesity. Type 2 diabetes. The list of struggles among American Catholics and non-Catholics is long. Each of these challenges is made more difficult by social isolation. And all of them could be alleviated, at least somewhat, by living in community with others. That is the life that Catholics have led for thousands of years. We support each other, at peace with God.

A few years ago, a mere three hundred feet from the front of our church, in a house directly across the street from the entrance to the Catholic school, a drug-related murder took place. Two people were shot, execution style, one of them fatally. This kind of thing isn't supposed to happen in a small town like ours, and yet it did. It outraged parishioners and the fearful parents of students, but the resentment was all directed outward.

Collectively, we were angry at slumlords, drug dealers, and the city government, who we blamed for allowing the neighborhood to fall apart. There was no talk about how we have turned our back on the same neighborhood, given up on the blocks surrounding our church. How we have systematically devalued this place through our actions. How we have signaled to everyone that, as Catholics, we think the best use of our neighbors' homes isn't to house our neighbors but to be razed for more parking.

We have not just walked away from the idea of the parish around our church. We have taken the next step and are now simply bad neighbors, accelerants of the decline we lament.

It is time for us to look beyond our walls and into the neighborhood we've done so much damage to. We need to put our energy into rebuilding the parish, the people in connection to the place.

"But where will I park?" In the list of urgent needs that stir our souls to action, this one seems out of place. Yet it is the practical need on the minds of those surrounding me in the pews. I love them, so let's deal with the parking issue and allow ourselves to move on to things that are worthy of our passion.

We have many elderly people, and others with physical limitations, who struggle to walk. They benefit from being able to park near the door. We also struggle to keep our youth fully engaged, to help them find a bridge between their immediate passions and a Catholic life of deep intention. These are struggles, but they are also gifts.

We can call on our youth to provide valet service for those in need. We can call on them to pick others up and transport them to Mass. If asked, they will do this with love and compassion, a step on their path of service within the community. Besides addressing the immediate physical need without further harm to the parish, the opportunity for both meaningful service and cross-generational fellowship is a gift we should not discount.

If we create such a program, we will no longer need the new parking we are planning to build, let alone the existing parking lots we've spent so much effort constructing. This land is better used for other things, so let's start making those things happen.

For example, our community needs housing. Let's build some. Our church bulletin is full of ads from local contractors, building supply companies, and realtors. We also have many people of means in our pews. Relying on the skills, talents, and capacity of our parishioners to build new housing around the church need not require a donation—it can be done profitably in a marketplace—but it can be done with Catholic sensibilities, the kind that glorifies the church and its environs.

We shouldn't stop with merely restoring our own parking lots. No, once we have repaired the harm we did to the neighborhood, we should turn our efforts to improving it, block by block. That will mean purchasing the drug house, and others around it, and fixing them up or replacing them. The neighborhood around our church should be the most beautiful, the most glorious, in the city, a place worthy of the Catholics who will be inspired to come back to the parish.

If people do wish to donate to this effort, that generosity can be turned into shelter for someone in distress—a parishioner needing to escape abuse, a family in need of temporary assistance, a mother who needs a break. We are Catholics. This is what we do.

Of course, with more parishioners living in the neighborhood, we will all have more opportunity to live an authentically Catholic life. That may mean bringing meals to that family in need or running a quick batch of cookies to the fellowship hall for a funeral. It could mean more people available to shovel snow in the winter and tend to the gardens in the summer, the latter an important need once we restore the St. Francis statue to its original location and then surround it with the magnificent landscaping the church deserves.

Localism

It will mean that, for many more people, daily Mass, holy hours, and adoration are but a short, healthy walk away, instead of a long, sedentary, and dangerous automobile trip. As we ponder Pope Francis's encyclical *Laudato Si*, we discover the many ways our own behavior and small choices can glorify God's creation.

Living side by side with other Catholics, instead of dispersed across the region, we will naturally discover many more opportunities for long walks, deep conversations, and other meaningful ways to support each other, at peace with God. Many people of faith crave such a community, not apart from American society but embedded firmly within it, a strong foundation of support for a life well-lived.

Our ancestors—Catholics, Protestants, and of those many other faiths around the world—built such communities from the bottom up. So can we. Doing so may be the most important work of our time.

Freedom Is in Our Pockets

JOSEPH PEARCE

That which is large enough for the rich to covet
… is large enough for the poor to defend.

—G. K. Chesterton

The Problem

At the beginning of chapter five of his best-selling book *Small Is Beautiful*, E. F. Schumacher discussed the political implications associated with scale. He had been brought up to believe the dogmatic assertion that the politics of scale were as inexorable and inevitable as the economies of scale and that history was determined by them. According to this determinist understanding of history, human political society began with the family; then families joined together to form tribes; then several tribes formed a nation; then a number of nations formed a "Union" or "United States" or "Empire"; finally, the consummation of this inexorable process would be the formation of a single world government. In my own book, *Small Is Still Beautiful*, I call this concept of political determinism the "theory of progressive centralization."

Anyone with a modicum of common sense will see that such a process signals the end of any meaningful representative government.

Localism

As government gets bigger, it gets further away from the people it governs, the latter of whom become practically powerless in political terms as impenetrable bureaucracies take control of their lives. This was the scenario envisaged by George Orwell in *Nineteen Eighty-Four*, in which the progressive centralization of power led to the world being divided between three empires or superpowers: Oceania, Eurasia, and Eastasia. In Orwell's time, the world was emerging from World War to Cold War and was seemingly merging into two Superpowers: the United States, with its NATO satellites, and the Soviet Union, with the slave-states it had brought into its orbit. Today we might see the world as being divided between four superpowers: the United States, China, the European Union, and Russia.

Yet this theory of progressive centralization is founded on the questionable assumption that a country or political state must be big to be prosperous. This conclusion, however, would appear to fly in the face of the known facts. Those small nations that refrained from joining the European Union, such as Switzerland and Norway, have done as well or better than similarly sized states that chose to surrender their sovereignty to the new European empire. The United Kingdom prospered when it chose to keep its national currency instead of sacrificing its fiscal freedom to the eurozone, despite the doomsday scenarios presented by those who believed that monetary union was essential to economic prosperity. Similarly, the U.K.'s decision to leave the E.U., known as "Brexit," did not lead to the economic meltdown that believers in the politics of scale predicted. Within the E.U., those small countries, such as Hungary, Poland, the Czech Republic, and Slovakia, which are resisting the imperialism of Brussels, are faring as well or better politically and economically than those nations that slavishly conform to the E.U.'s diktats.

As if the foregoing were not enough to cast serious doubt on the theory of progressive centralization, the success of the numerous small states that emerged after the break-up of the Soviet Union should confirm that small nations can thrive and survive in the modern world. And what is true of nation-states is equally true of the individual states within the United States, many of which are as large or larger than European nations and with comparable populations. The return to such local government of the vast power usurped by the Federal Government would benefit the people in those localities economically, as well as liberating them politically.

There is, however, one other aspect of the theory of progressive centralization that has only emerged in recent years with the advent of technologically driven globalism. How does this push toward a globalized hegemony, ushered in by the unholy alliance of big tech, big business, and big government, impact the viability of local businesses and local cultures? Can the small, local, and beautiful survive and prosper in a world dominated by the big, global, and brash?

Whether we are talking of small nations in a globalized world or small businesses in a globalized market, the problem is essentially the same. Can these human-scale political and economic entities survive? This is the problem. What follows will be practical suggestions toward making the answer to that question a resoundingly emphatic "Yes"!

The Solution

The first thing necessary for the solution to the problem of progressive centralization is the acceptance that there is a solution. Failure to act on the basis that nothing can be done is abject surrender to the powers of tyranny. Doing nothing in such circumstances is what we might call the Denethor Option.

Denethor is the character in *The Lord of the Rings* who spends too much time staring into the *palantír* stone, which is the Middle-earth equivalent of the computer screen. Those who look into these stones receive the latest "news" of what's happening in the world. The problem is that the news is provided by the dominant will who controls the stones, so that a steady stream of propaganda is shown to the viewer. The dominant will who controls the stones is the demonic Sauron, who shows Denethor that the powers of evil are so mighty that it is futile to resist their inevitable victory. Believing the propaganda, Denethor refuses to take practical steps to defend his civilization from the evil forces advancing upon it, choosing instead to commit suicide in an act of despair.

Doing nothing is not an option.

So what is to be done?

The answer is very close to home. It's so close to home that it's actually in our pockets.

The bottom line is that every dollar we spend is a vote that we cast for a better or a worse world. Dollars are the weapons with which the culture wars will be won or lost: not someone else's dollars but our own. The buck stops with each one of us, which means, to mess with the idiom, that we need to pass the buck to the right people.

There will be no revival of strong local government until there is a revival of strong local economies and strong local cultures. And we, as individuals and families, are the key to building these economies and cultures.

Having established the principles, the remainder of what follows will be a practical guide to voting with our dollars on a daily basis to build a better world.

Beginning with one of the timeless foundations of culture, the imbibing of fermented and distilled beverages, we should buy locally produced craft ales, beers, wines, and spirits. The proliferation of local craft breweries, wineries, and distilleries has been a very healthy development in recent years, indicative of the desire for local culture. We should buy these beverages instead of the globally branded products. If they cost more, we should either spend more or drink less. Every dollar spent on a locally crafted beverage is building a better world. Every dollar spent on the mass-produced equivalents is building a globalist future for ourselves and our children.

Moving to another timeless foundation of culture, the art of eating well, we should buy our meat and produce, insofar as we can, directly from local producers and farmers. Avoid the supermarkets, especially the global or national chains, and go to the farmers' markets instead. Insofar as we do use large-scale grocery stores, we need to be aware of the corporate mission statement. Does the corporation advocate the globalist agenda or other political ideologies that are harmful to the strong family life that is the very foundation of healthy local culture? If so, don't make the world a worse place by casting your monetary vote for such policies by spending your money in those places.

With respect to knowing which corporations are poisonous and which are less so, localists should form organizations and provide information aimed at exposing bad companies, which are part of the problem, and also highlight those good companies that are helping to promote healthier local culture. Does a national or global chain sell local produce, for instance? Beware. Be aware.

Try to minimize the number of dollars we spend on the products of global corporations. Since hi-tech products are connected to the globalist hegemony, try to become a techno-minimalist. Use technology as little as you can. Spend as little money as you can on it. Disconnect from the globalist network so that you can reconnect locally.

If you need work done on your property, look for local businesses, not larger companies. Avoid the ads placed at the top of internet search pages by the biggest companies and scroll down to the local businesses.

Eat at locally owned restaurants, not chains. Attend performances by local theater companies. Remove your children from the public school system, which advocates globalism and other harmful ideologies. Enroll them in small, local schools, especially classical academies, or, if you can, take the radical step of homeschooling them.

These are just a few practical guidelines for making the world a better place with every dollar we spend. We can't make a perfect world, but we can make it better. We can't defeat the devil, but we can defy him.

And speaking of the devil, we don't need to defeat him, not merely because he has already been defeated by Christ, but because he is always defeating himself. Pride precedes a fall, and the devil is such a fool that he always proceeds to the fall that follows hard on the heels of his pride. And what is true of the devil is equally true of his advocates. Ultimately, any political, economic, or social system rooted in pride and obsessive "empowerment" is doomed to self-destruct. Globalism is unsustainable.

The culture of death is not only deadly but suicidal. It will kill itself. In the meantime, the living dead, like the poor, are always with us. Let them get on with their own ultimately self-defeating plans. As for the rest of us, we can begin by loving our neighbors in the literal sense of supporting our local communities and local cultures.

It might be true that we can't make Heaven on earth, but we can get to Heaven by making our own corner of earth a better place.

If we want freedom, we need only to reach in our pockets. We have nothing to lose but our chains and our loose change.

The Localist Mind

Fr. Michael Rennier

When I arrived at Epiphany of Our Lord parish in St. Louis, Missouri, five years ago as the new pastor, I inherited a sanctuary that had been emptied. The entire plain, curved wall of the forty-foot-tall apse in the Romanesque building had been painted beige. All of it. The tiled floor was beige. The altar was off-white marble. A wooden cross, the only art in the sanctuary, dangled over the altar on four wires. A dark-gray corpus hung upon it, and there was not even a speck of color to define the features on Our Lord's face.

The priest prior to me attempted to fix the yawning void—for which he was not responsible—by hanging factory-produced colored banners and keeping flowers in the vicinity of the altar. Still, the sanctuary felt like a chasm. The parishioners hated it.

Our modest-sized parish didn't have great riches to throw at a professional fix. That wasn't a problem, though, because for generations, the Catholic faithful have dedicated themselves to beautifying their houses of worship. Everyday craftsmen, artisans, carpenters, and masons have raised entire cathedrals like jewels in the middle of farming villages. While it's true that few of us have mastery of sacred arts such as mural-painting, gold-leafing, or creating statuary, there's an entire mid-level of decorative arts that, with dedication and practice, is well within reach. I'm thinking, for example, about embroidery, sewing, carpentry, and calligraphy.

I located a parishioner with graphic design skills and asked him to design visually interesting, non-cartoonish banners to adorn the walls until such a day as we could hire professional painters. This he gladly did. I asked another parishioner to sew tabernacle veils and frontals for the altar. They look lovely, drawing the eye to the center of the space and dressing the altar in noble vestments. We obtained a *fleur-de-lis* stencil, and a parishioner helped me paint the (beige) walls behind our St. Thérèse and St. Anthony statues with a blue and gold pattern. A friend of mine, a philosophy professor, handcrafted a wooden prie-dieu wide enough for two parishioners to kneel and receive Communion. A homeschool girl embroidered a gorgeous sacred heart onto the hood of a cope. Another teen girl hand-drew and illustrated a set of prayer cards for the sacristy. A friend of mine, Maggie, had gone to a vestment-making retreat with the Benedictine sisters. I commissioned set after set of new vestments from her that we designed together.

The change was palpable. It felt as though God Himself had breathed into the space. What had been formless and void sprang into full flower.

All of this arising from the labor of parishioners, amateurs each one in their contributions, who love the church and desire to clothe her in beauty.

❖ ❖ ❖

For many years, I considered myself a minimalist. With the heady brashness of youth, I derided the cult of consumerism, vowing to divest of all material clutter and acquisitiveness. I avoided big-box stores and eliminated as much interaction as I could with globalist corporations. I didn't want to support them with my business and felt like Judas when I did.

I owned very few items of clothing, and all were purchased at a thrift store. The furniture in my first apartment was fished out of dumpsters. I desired to be pure intellect. Pure spirit. Material things were an obstacle to that goal. I was the sort of person who theoretically would have loved that blank, empty sanctuary at Epiphany parish.

In his autobiography, G. K. Chesterton mentions a similar unease with large corporate structures, writing, "If my father had been some common millionaire owning a thousand mills that made cotton, or a million machines that made cocoa, how much smaller he would have seemed.... The manufacturer cannot even manufacture things; he can only pay to have them manufactured." His main complaint is that large-scale manufacturing destroys creativity. It separates us from the human vocation to be *makers*, to create in imitation of the way God creates. His breath, remember, is our breath.

Chesterton and I share the same concern about consumerism, but as a young man I dealt with it differently. I defined myself by what I avoided. I dreamed of boycotting everything and having nothing. Chesterton, on the other hand, wasn't avoiding. He was seeking. He sought to rediscover the beauty of creativity. He admired how his father created amateur works of art for the walls of their home, how he made toys for his children, how he built a *home*.

My mistake was to misunderstand thriftiness, the idea of keeping my interior space uncluttered and free of a wasteful, consumerist mentality. I'd become a minimalist miser, throwing everything that was beautiful away from myself in a rash attempt to free myself from consumerism. I became an empty sanctuary. A void. Still, for many more years, I held my breath.

Chesterton breathes more freely. Thrift, as he explains in *What's Wrong with the World*, isn't purposeful lack. It isn't a ruthless clean sweep. Rather, thrift is a rejection of blind consumerism in order to protect what is truly useful, good, and beautiful. Thrift nurtures creativity and fashions a beauty all its own. "If a man could undertake to make use of all the things in his dustbin," says Chesterton, "He would be a broader genius than Shakespeare."

There's genius in how my parishioners have beautified their church through creative thrift. There's intentionality of purpose in their sacred, made objects, a devotional power that shines through. In my experience, Chesterton's statement that, "Thrift is poetic because it is creative," is very much true. We're still working on beautifying our parish, but the air now positively hums with poetic energy. When I arrived, it felt like a building. Now it feels like a spiritual home.

❖ ❖ ❖

Across the Mississippi River from St. Louis is the town of Cahokia, Illinois. French missionaries from Quebec arrived in Cahokia on December 8, 1698, and offered the Holy Sacrifice of the Mass on the banks of the Mississippi River, which at that time was known as the River of the Immaculate Conception. I've stood in that same spot and touched the Missal those priests used. I opened it to the Mass for the day they used, the Mass for the Conception of the Blessed Virgin Mary. It just so happens to be the same feast day on which I was ordained to the priesthood. These are miraculous acts of creativity on the part of our Heavenly Father. First, the Real Presence on the shore of the river among the aromatic sumac and primrose. No less so, generations later, the creation of a priest for His Church.

This is where Holy Family was built. Lovingly referred to as the Log Church, it's the oldest church west of the Allegheny

Mountains. Made of black walnut timbers stacked *poteaux-en-terre* and still in use today, it's an example of the American frontier spirit. You can still go there to pray or view the beautiful vestments and dignified sanctuary with its high altar. Some of the items inside—ciboria, monstrance, candlesticks—are imported from Europe, gifts from various French monarchs, but much of it is handmade. The timbers were cut and milled on site. Lanterns, altar, sacristy, all made and gifted by local Catholics. How much beauty in that house of prayer is the work of rough, calloused hands that lived on the opposite bank of the river from me some two hundred years ago.

❖ ❖ ❖

I'm a convert to Catholicism. Ordained a pastor in the Anglican tradition in 2006, and received into full communion with the Catholic Church in 2010, I'm now an ordained, happily married Catholic priest. We have six children still living at home. We curate our domestic budget carefully.

I'm a different man now than I was in my youth. I now desire a beautiful home, not an empty one. However, in some ways, I'm still the same. I still decline to spend money with large corporations if I can avoid it. I still avoid the empty promises of shopping-therapy and debt-funded acquisitiveness. The idea of wastefulness galls me. I'm the type of father who walks circuits in the house multiple times per day flipping the light switches off in empty rooms.

For any family, thrift is a necessary virtue. It helps us locate the mean between consumerism and anti-materialism. I'm a big fan of William Morris, the English designer and poet who was influential in founding the Arts and Crafts movement in the second half of the nineteenth century. Morris summarized his philosophy as, "Have nothing in your house that you do not know to be beautiful, or believe to be useful." In other words, thrift is beauty and beauty is thrift.

Chesterton was quite familiar with Morris. The Victorian era in which he grew up was heavily influenced by the great designer. In his book of collected essays, *Twelve Types*, he dedicates a full essay to Morris. He admires Morris, writing, "He represents also that honorable instinct for finding beauty in common necessities of workmanship which gives it a stronger and more bony structure." He notes, however, that Morris has his limitations, namely, that in rejecting the ugly and wasteful consumerism of industrial England, he buries himself in a romanticized vision of the past. The two men are firmly bonded, though, in their refusal to accept ugliness or waste. Chesterton is positively mystified at how bad it had become, writing, "It is indeed difficult to account for the clinging curse of ugliness which blights everything brought forth by the most prosperous of centuries."

Morris, for all the good he did in making beauty possible in ordinary homes, perhaps retreated too far into an idyllic past. Chesterton counsels creativity better integrated with hopefulness—thrift for the present age. In his autobiography, he mentions that his family took the Arts and Crafts movement to an extreme by hand-crafting their own decorations. "I am now incurably afflicted with a faint smile," he writes, "when I hear a crowd of frivolous people, who could not make anything to save their lives, talking about the inevitable narrowness and stuffiness of the Victorian home. We managed to make a good many things in our Victorian home which people now buy at insane prices from Art and Craft Shops." Note carefully what he says. His childhood home didn't suffer from the stuffiness of a typical home in which the decorations are curated from catalogs because, by spurring creativity, thrift filled the house with beauty.

I try to fill our home, too, with beautiful, handmade objects, each one the product of thrifty genius. My wife re-upholsters furniture and patches chipped porcelain lamps back together. We found a lovely, old dining room table in a second-hand shop and refinished it. Our piano was given to us by my grandmother. Books that have been read many times are stacked in piles, adding color to shelves and end tables. The walls are adorned with art made by family members, including framed embroideries and watercolors of native flowers. We have some nice things—I like to poke around the local antique shop from time to time—but very little that has been mass-produced, and no one would accuse us of being hoarders.

Outside, my boys hammer together make-shift ramps for their skateboards and disappear into the garage with their grandfather to emerge triumphantly with new sleds built with his assistance. They make armor out of cardboard and weaponry out of sticks and rubber bands. In the kitchen, the culinary arts are distinctly local and creative as well. Our meat comes from a local farmer, our raw milk from another. We buy local produce from a co-op. We don't eat in chain restaurants, vastly preferring to prepare our own feasts. I roast my own coffee beans. My daughters bake banana bread and apple pies. One daughter interns for a local artist. Another works for a family-run knife sharpening business. Before that, they worked for a family-run business that helped people keep chickens in their backyard.

We prefer to buy from people we know. Our philosophy is that their goods are crafted with more love and thus are higher quality. We know that, unlike globalist corporations, they aren't using their operating budget to donate to causes we find morally questionable.

Our thrifty habits are more than an economic choice. We have set ourselves free to be creative, to pour love into the objects we choose to surround ourselves with. The pictures on the wall, the food we eat, the clothes we wear, none of it was made to impress or corner an economic market. These items we've bought locally or crafted ourselves have an energy, a directness, that's lacking in objects made by nameless machines in far-away factories. These locally sourced objects were made by hands that know what they're about. Even if they're less shiny and trendy, they surpass anything in a glossy magazine. They are the result of love. The items I treasure most were all made by my wife or children.

❖ ❖ ❖

I've come to understand that I need to love things more, not less. In this regard, consumerists and anti-materialists are working from the same playbook. Both oppose ascribing value to a physical object. The consumerist thinks it's disposable, and the anti-materialist refuses to see the good in it to start with. God, however, clearly loves and values His creation. The care with which He instructs the Israelites in the decoration of His Temple is a case in point.

The answer to consumerism is moderation and love: moderation in consumption and genuine love of beautiful objects. The two work together, for we only bestow love on that which is worthy. A person who loves objects for their intrinsic goodness will not consent to be surrounded by mass-produced baubles and will not wastefully throw out items simply because they've lost sheen. But such a person will happily surround himself with beautiful things, will be inspired by these beautiful things, may even seek to create or obtain additional beautiful things.

Thrift, in the Chestertonian sense, reveals that handmade and local isn't replaceable. All the money in the world cannot force a factory to fashion an object with love. My teenaged daughter, however, can easily and happily create an item made with love.

William Morris was a great admirer of the medieval churches of England because they were built by local craftsmen as an act of love. The stones of such churches cry out with the devotion of their builders. Morris particularly loved the little parish church in Kelmscott near his country house. Of the decoration inside, he says, "These are the works of the Thames-side country bumpkins, as you would call us — nothing grander than that."

Concern over the cost of globalist consumerism doesn't mean we must throw our hands up in frustration and have nothing. It means we get to have everything. Through thrift, a world of creativity opens up. Creativity seeks beauty. It's a poetic act that expresses the simple, irrevocable blessedness of existing: that it is good to live on this planet so overshadowed by God's love and occupy ourselves in the creation of beautiful, useful objects that reflect His love. This is domestic bliss, this beauty that draws down God into our homes and hearts.

Chesterton was a man who knew that absolutely anything, with a little thrift and creativity, can be a work of art. One of my favorite essays he wrote is about a piece of chalk that, on a whim, he takes into a field to spend the morning drawing. After happily sketching for a while, his chalk breaks, leaving him sad he cannot complete his picture. Suddenly, he laughs. He has remembered he's sitting in the countryside in southern England. Every single rock poking through the turf is made of chalk.

Friends, let out a slow breath, break off a piece of chalk, and draw.

The American Idyll

E. WESLEY REYNOLDS III

Woe unto them that join house to house,
that lay field to field, till there be no place,
that they may be placed alone
in the midst of the earth!

—Isaiah 5:8

When I ask my students, "What does one square mile mean to you?" a blank stare usually follows. Technology serves them for what land served their great grandfathers.

It was once considered our national story that people came to the North American continent in search for land to make a home, but land meant so much more to our ancestors than it generally does to us now. In a world without electric lights, instant communication, and infrastructure, the home rested on a balance of natural life inside and around it. In Paradise, it was גַּן, or Garden; after the Fall, it become הַֽדֶּשׁ, χωράφι, *hortus*, the pastoral idyll.

America's ancestors knew that the only means of establishing a people is to root them into the land without destroying it, that is, begin a *pastoral*. On this point, the pilgrims, pioneers, and poets of America all agreed. For one thing, all read the same Bible with its pastoral patriarchs, shepherd kings, and prophets of the wildernesses. By the late nineteenth century, most of America's educated populace read very deeply the Greek and Roman pastoral poets. All knew Merrie Olde England and its celebration of free yeoman life. But in America, the pastoral idyll took shape more freely than in Europe, because land was not all in the hands of corrupt, profiteering landlords. American settlers would not have considered America "new" in the contemporary sense of the word. They called America "new" because it would be a return to an old idyll, fresh and ready. America would primarily validate the rights of the freeholders, the yeoman of a "new England." As this hope grew, so did the cultural beauty of the ideal. The pioneers carried the pleasures of field, pasture, and the hunt deep into the forests of America. The American poets forever memorialized a frontier world that would soon shrink before the advent of commercial agriculture and finally industrialization. Still, Americans were slow to embrace the change, and most of its lower-class population preferred the homespun subsistence of America's prairies to the wage-labor system emerging in the East.

Pastoral life, as understood by the ancients, depends upon a balance between tilled farmland, open pastureland, and unbounded forests and mountains. Unlike agrarianism, pastoral idylls did not insist on the monopoly of the field. Unlike environmentalism, the spiritual landscape of the Psalms, the idylls of Theocritus and Horace, and the *Metamorphoses* of Ovid all emphasize a proper sphere of human cultivation inside a much larger natural order. Nature contained a proper sphere for every being, both spiritually and geographically. Man might violate his sphere, but there was no competition between man and nature, only conflicts between various flawed passions in nature.

Pastoral poetry ultimately evokes the *Logos* to so order a local world according to a variety of being: a validation of beast, tree, field, stone, water, light, dark, wind, sea, etc., all in their proper spheres and limits. In the cottage and tilled field grew the "vine and fig tree," or the fruit of one's labor so celebrated in America. In the open pastureland lived the shepherd "beside the still waters." And in the wilds were the delights of hunt and dance. The great *not-man* lurked in the forests or wastes beyond the pasture, but the grandeur of such a natural order sustained man's place inside it with game for the hunt, streams of water, and solitary haunts for prayer. If one cut down the trees, man lost his solitary retreats and his sustenance in times of famine. If one burned the fields, men fled to the woods and became savage. If one enslaved the shepherds and enclosed the common lands, men became tenants to oppressive landowners. Truth, beauty, and goodness resided in all three spheres of earth. So the ancient poets had it.

And so the Pilgrims articulated it on the shores of America. The Pilgrims are often represented as either radical early capitalists, establishing private property in America, or else stern killers of indigenous peoples and fellers of forests. They were, in fact, simply free Christian yeomen of England who came to enjoy in peace and liberty the pleasures of the family altar, field, and hunt. The hunt played a significant role in the imagination of the Plymouth Pilgrims. In fact, the First Thanksgiving was just that; a thankful celebration of God's plenty in both field and wood. Their relations with the indigenous hunters and planters in America and their respect for the limits between field and wood helped them achieve a pastoral idyll that was unknown in England, where forests were scarce and reserved for the upper classes. In the only direct account left behind of the First Thanksgiving, Edward Winslow describes it thus:

Our corn did prove well, and God be praised ... our harvest
being gotten in, our governor sent four men on fowling,
that so we might after a special manner rejoice together
... at which time amongst other recreations, we exercised
our arms, and many of the Indians coming amongst us ...
Massasoit, with some ninety men, whom for three days we
entertained and feasted, and they went out and killed five
deer, which they brought to the Plantation.

Similarly, Bradford's entire account of Plymouth is framed by a
"vine and fig tree" image, where the harvest and hunt play equal
roles in the communal life of the colony. Man was to be half *ager*
and half *silva*. They had left Holland for no other reason. Bradford
wrote: "Being now come to the Low Countries [the Netherlands],
they saw many goodly and fortified cities ... strange fashions and at-
tires; all so far differing from that of their plain country villages....
Some preferred and chose the prisons of England, rather than the
liberties of Holland."

The Pilgrims were escaping commerce and spiritual materialism of cities as much as they were fleeing persecution. They hoped
that their covenant faithfulness to God would lead to blessings on
their descendants forever.

So also did Governor John Winthrop of Massachusetts Bay
swear an oath to God and with all the people saying, "Soe that
if wee shall deale falsely with our God in this worke wee haue
undertaken ... Wee shall open the mouthes of enemies to speake
evill of the wayes of God ... till wee be consumed out of the good
land whither wee are a goeing."

What of the Puritan's aversion to country revels and the folk
entertainments of Europe? Did they not utterly reject as sinful the
village maypole, the pantomime, the feast day, the playhouse, and

the Morris dance? Certainly. But their sometimes superstitious fear of such things came from exactly the same source. It was because the Puritans were so pastoral in their imagination that they feared witchcraft and denounced the ritualistic. Their pastoral musings were those of David the Psalmist, not of Bacchus the reveler, but perhaps they feared the night a little too much.

New England grew around little congregational towns with farmers nestled between great expanses of forests and long coastal areas bustling with fisheries. Because of their social, geographical, and bio-diversity, New Englanders developed localized trades and divided their time between village crafts, farming, hunting, and fishing. Because of these decentralized sources of wealth, artisans were freer to adapt to their local climates than in large cities where guilds still controlled crafts like glassblowing, silversmithing, and cabinetry. Still, New England's cities excelled in these trades as well, and by the end of the eighteenth century, the region had matured into a very prosperous and balanced pre-industrialized economy.

After its Great Awakening, New England maintained its pastoral spirituality in its Christian hymnody. England's Isaac Watts became America's poet laureate, and his hymn "Jesus Shall Reign" is a particularly appropriate sample of pastoral feeling:

> To Him shall endless prayer be made,
> and praises throng to crown His head.
> His name like sweet perfume shall rise
> with every morning sacrifice.

In contrast to New England's pastoral variety, the southern gentry bought up land in large parcels, mostly in the tidewater region of Virginia and Maryland. Tobacco not only dominated the agrarian economy of the early South but created a culture all its own in which status and wealth were closely tied to the quality of tobacco varieties. Under Governor Berkeley's leadership, planters gained complete control of the government and began taxing the yeomanry through heavy land rents. In 1676, Nathaniel Bacon led a farmers' revolt against the government at Jamestown and burned the city to the ground in protest. After that, the Virginian yeomanry gained back their political rights, but the agrarian South never managed to diversify its local sources of wealth so as to avoid the commercialization of agriculture. Exporting crops became the Deep South's primary occupation. Only in the frontier forests of the Upper South and Northwest, where the clannish descendants of Scots-Irish settlers built log cabins in the hollows and hills of the Appalachian mountains, was there any vestige of a pastoral southern way of life. Perhaps this is why America's poets all looked to the North and West for their pastoral inspiration.

America's pioneers took the pastoral imagination further west, but also brought about its eventual destruction by laying waste to the hunting lands, transitioning toward commercial agriculture, and insisting on the removal of Native Americans in the frontier. Still, most pioneers were hunter-farmers up through the 1840s and the advent of canals and railroads. Their world was a "middle ground" of hunting, fur trading, planting, harvesting, and canoeing. As more and more towns sprouted near midwestern waterways, a seasonal life emerged that, as many prints from the era show, celebrated a life of cidering, corn-husking, and barn-raising. This was no easy life, and only after thirty years of hard work could any realistic pioneer expect a successful homestead. Accounts like William Nowlin's *The Bark Covered House*, Alexis De Tocqueville's *A Fortnight in the Wilderness*, and Laura Ingalls Wilder's semi-autobiographical Little House series attest to the fact that a mixture of hunting, trapping, planting, and crafts were absolutely necessary to survive the desolate openness of the frontier. Still, pioneers felled more trees than they planted.

McCormick's reaper, Eli Whitney's cotton gin, the commercialization of agriculture, the national politicization of internal improvements, and finally the removal of American Indians made this diversification less and less possible. As railroads swept up all the freight along the interior, logging companies bought out all the large forests. Farmers were forced to depend on the crop-lien system to supply them with seed, and American agriculture across the South and Midwest sunk into a debt cycle from which it could not naturally emerge. The Grange, Farmers Alliances, and finally the formation of the Populist Party substituted agrarian reaction for pastoral conservation. America had replaced its pastoral frontier with an agrarian ideal that was unrealistic and unsustainable, and it eventually gave way to the industrialization of agriculture and urbanization.

Yet even as the contradictions in pioneer life emerged, America's rural poets still celebrated America as the "new world" of pastoral imagination. That literary tradition began with three writers who set the tone for American's pastoral poets.

James Fenimore Cooper's *Pathfinder* and *Last of the Mohicans* set the American pioneer inside a vanishing frontier, one in which the hunt and the homestead sat sometimes at odds and sometimes at unity with each other. He gave America a haunting fascination for the woods in ways that no Emerson or Thoreau, with all their introspective philosophy, could ever fully realize.

Washington Irving worked in the opposite direction, depicting in his "sketches" the remnants of "times wild and picturesque" that were hidden away in the wholesome rural customs of the many hamlets that dotted the American and European landscapes.

Irving took Americans back to their hearths and pastures to find wholesome revel in the seasons.

Hawthorn imbued the hamlet with a darker mysticism. His idealized Puritan world of midnight witching bonfires, secret fears, and moral examinations contrasted the stifling village with America's unbounded landscape.

The thematic pallet of these writers of America's forests became the colors that four great American poets mixed to form the American pastoral idyll: Henry Wadsworth Longfellow, John Greenleaf Whittier, Oliver Wendell Holmes, and James Whitcomb Riley.

It would be a gross error to reduce the vast work of these poets down to an exclusively agrarian ideal. Plowing occupies very little room in these poems, and when it does, it is usually equated with life's toils rather than with vigor or beauty. The orchard features more prominently in images of the American homestead and its seasonal life. Drovers, fishermen, lumbermen, and corn-huskers people this little world. Upon the hilltops, winds from under mountain shadows and eastern seacoasts sweep down into village orchards where lovers, schoolboys, and rovers wander. Old inns stand ready to receive wayworn travelers, and windmills overlook meadows where "across the road the barns display their lines of stalls, their mows of hay." Both Whittier and Holmes repeatedly represented the thanksgiving harvest of the Pilgrims as an initiating pageant in which America's sacred landscape transformed itself into a fruitful "Western Palestine."

Further up, into the unbounded mountains and forests overlooking every village, cataracts of water leap from stone to stone, and every spring flower, every summer blossom, every autumn vine links itself in a pastoral dance of majesty and prosperity. America's golden autumns hold a special significance for Longfellow, Whittier, and Holmes, in which crisp, sublime color preserves forever the memory of youthful springs long gone. In all, the interplay between forest, mountain, and field nourishes the vibrant lives of America's growing population.

There is in these poems a consistent lamentation for a world that the poets believed was passing from the American scene. Whittier expressed it thus:

> Against the wooded hills it stands,
> Ghosts of a dead home, stealing through
> Its broken lights on wasted lands
> Where old-time harvests grew.
>
> Gone the winter's sleet and snowing,
> Gone the spring-time's bud and blowing,
> Gone the summer's harvest moving,
> And again the fields are gray.

Old time used to remember the beauty of the woods, or the "patriarch of the primal wood," where "In simpler days of the world's early childhood, men crowned with garlands, gifts, and praise such monarchs of the wild-wood.... When winds shake down his winter snow in silver avalanches." This was what was meant by Longfellow's *Song of Hiawatha* or Holmes "Even Song" or "No Time like Old Time."

But poetry cannot ever be summarized; rarely can it be analyzed without destroying its beauty. It must be lived, as it was lived by generations of boys and girls in the country schoolyards, where schoolmistresses kept the gates of fairyland with the watchwords from a thousand seasonal poems that formed the pageant of all our outdoor games and heroic songs. This is what called Dorothy back from Oz again. It is what kept Rebecca on her sunny brook farm. It is why "Curly" sings "Oh, What a Beautiful Mornin'" and also why Joe tragically sings "Ol' Man River." It is why Copland wrote "Appalachian Spring," why Katherine Lee Bates wrote "America the Beautiful" and Sammy Fain wrote of the "picket fence and rambling rose" in "Dear Hearts and Gentle People." It is what reminded Whitcomb Riley of the "Whistling Boy," the frost on the pumpkin, "The Old Swimmin'-Hole" "the same old summer with the same old smile," "the honeysuckles, midst the hollyhocks, that clamber almost to the martin-box," and "The Orchard Lands of Long Ago."

But Riley was late. After 1900, the Indiana that he remembered was almost a thing of the past, and soon the pastoral world would vanish before a new "American Dream," which we instinctively believed to be more real than our earlier lives. Our old loves were forgotten, nay dismissed as fantom dreams that made the drudgery of our primitive lives bearable until we found more modern conveniences. If we are ever to reclaim simplicity, locality, and beauty in America, we should start by reading our pastoral poets, pilgrims, and pioneers and rebuild their hearthstone.

Appendix: Ancient and American Pastoral Poetry

Please note, a reading of the inspired Hebrew Scriptures and of the "lower" Greek mythology with its poets of local haunts is necessary to recover the pastoral imagination. Folklore and lower mythologies were read by most liberally educated students until modern classicists rooted them out in favor of the higher mythologies and cosmological dramas of Mount Olympus in Homer and Virgil. Citations of the lesser poets, such as Horace and Ovid, abound among the London writers and American Founders of the eighteenth century. Furthermore, the European populous had long incorporated many Roman and Germanic domestic pastoral rites into the holiday revels and Christian feast days of their many varied hamlets.

The Reformation and the age of sociability that followed it in the seventeenth and eighteenth centuries allegorized the pastoral elements of the Classical world, purging it of its paganism. The muses, graces, fauns, pans, groves, and local geniuses of hill and lake became adjectives that substituted the ontological claims of pagan myth with stylistic allegory. This even extended to the Olympians; hence the rise in popularity of anthropomorphic characteristics such as "saturnine," "mercurial," and "jovial" among the early English novelists, commentators, and critics until a sharp decline in such Olympian terminology after the 1850s. Romanticism rejected this sort of classicism and elevated instead the pastoral motifs into spiritual faculties without considering them metaphysical realities. Romantics also mixed the Greek and Roman idylls with Persian and Turkish folklore, as in Shelley's *Hellas* and Byron's *The Bride of Abydos*. To the lower Greek mythology may be added the Celtic and Norse bardic tradition, which was late in coming to European and American literature.

America is unique in preserving a purified Hebraism in its folklore, celebrating the Psalms and the Nativity of Christ over the Greek idylls. The Hebraic influence runs even through the American Romantic poets who introduced lower Greek festivity into American folklore. The Hudson River School artists also depicted America as a western Palestine and a western Arcadia. The Puritan and Congregationalist sources of this peculiarly American form of pastoral piety are not represented here, as they are not strictly poetic. For more than a century and a half after its initial settlement, America imported its poetry, hymnody, and even much of its folklore. The poetic urge in American literature was not fully felt until after the romantic fascination for all things "picturesque"; or those remnants of European and Native American civilizations that lingered on in obscure corners of the pastoral American landscape.

Localism

The principal American poetry alluded to in this piece includes:

❖ Longfellow, Henry Wadsworth. *The Complete Poetical Works of Henry Wadsworth Longfellow, Cambridge Edition*. Boston and New York: Houghton, Mifflin and Company, 1900.

"The Bridge of Cloud"
"The Brook and the Wave"
"A Day of Sunshine"
"Hawthorne"
"In the Harbor"
"My Lost Youth"
"The New England Tragedies"
"Tales of a Wayside Inn"
"The Windmill"
"Weariness"

❖ Whittier, John Greenleaf. *The Complete Poetical Works of John Greenleaf Whittier, Household Edition*. Boston and New York: Houghton, Mifflin and Company, 1894.

"Autumn Thoughts"
"Birchbrook Mill"
"The Bridal of Pennacook"
"Channing"
"Corn-Song"
"Dedication"
"A Dream of Summer"
"Drovers"
"The Familist's Hymn"
"Fishermen"
"For an Autumn Festival"
"The Funeral Tree of the Sokokis"

"The Golden Wedding of Longwood"
"Gone"
"Hazel Blossoms"
"The Hill-Top"
"The Homestead"
"Huskers"
"In School-Days"
"The Lake-Side"
"The Laurels"
"Lumbermen"
"The Mayflowers"
"Mogg Megone"
"My Playmate"
"An Outdoor Reception"
"The Pennsylvania Pilgrim"
"The Prophecy of Samuel Sewall"
"The Pumpkin"
"To Delaware"
"Seed-Time and Harvest"
"Summer"
"A Summer Pilgrimage"
"Summer's Day Excursion"
"The Ranger"
"Vesta"
"The Wood Giant"

❖ Holmes, Oliver Wendell. *The Complete Poetical Works of Oliver Wendell Holmes, Cambridge Edition.* Boston and New York, Houghton, Mifflin and Company, 1895.

   "The Golden Flower"
   "In the Twilight"

"The New Eden"
"Our Indian Summer"
"The Pilgrim's Vision"
"Poetry: A Metrical Essay"
"The Wood Giant"

❖ Riley, James Whitcomb. *The Complete Works of James Whitcomb Riley*. New York: Harper and Brothers Publishers, 1916.

"An Old Friend"
"The Old Swimmin'-Hole"
"The Orchard Lands of Long Ago"
"To a Boy Whistling"
"We Must Get Home"
"When the Frost is on the Punkin'"

Taste and See

CARMEL RICHARDSON

My husband likes to joke that the best restaurant in the world is Chili's. It started because he does in fact like the place, but it has continued because he likes even better to rib his wife—and because she takes the bait every time.

I take it for the obvious reason: restaurants like Chili's are, objectively, a complete waste of space. You are startled that I take such a hard line on Chili's, but you won't be once you begin to think about it. Its very lack of remarkability is one of its chief offenses. I've eaten Mexican food of higher quality from a food truck and paid half the amount I would for Chili's weekly dinner specials.

But let us be fair. Chili's is only doing exactly what O'Charley's did for steakhouses, and Olive Garden for real Italian, and it is doing it quite successfully too. Such mid-level chains do not exist to provide exquisite food. They do not seek to be the very cheapest thing you can find to eat, either; McDonald's already cornered that market. Instead, they offer food that is passing fair at a price that is decently affordable. In today's inflated economy, that's often cheaper than a home-cooked meal, though only by a margin.

These restaurants proliferate across middle America. There is hardly an interstate exit in the Southeast or Midwest without at least one, never mind the mecca that is Breezewood, Pennsylvania. This makes a reliably mediocre sit-down dinner also a quick and convenient stopping point on a road trip or a regular night in Small Town, U.S.A. That's the point. In short, the marginal economies of price and time are worth, to a plurality of Americans, the economy of flavor.

So we might call Chili's smart, because it saw a niche in the market and captured it. But "smart" and "good" are two different things. Chili's is not good. And I will tell you why.

In his cookbook-meets-theological musing, *The Supper of the Lamb*, Episcopal priest Robert Farrar Capon makes the distinction between festal and ferial food. The ferial is short on expense but high on creativity. It is the leg of lamb that is stretched across four meals by using each of its parts to the utmost: roasted as a main course, bones for broth, less desirable cuts for stew, scraps turned into casseroles or fried rice. It is efficient, but it is also excellent. Festal food, meanwhile, spares no dollar; it is lavish, and appropriately so, made for feast days as it were. Both are fitting for their seasons, but what is inappropriate—and, for Capon, even a transgressive use of the culinary arts—is to reduce food to an economy of time or space. There are several ways to do this: one is to count calories; another is to wish to do away with the serious work of curating, cooking, and cleaning that are involved in both festal and ferial dining. Both turn dining into something purely utilitarian, rather than an art or even an act of worship. Thus, concludes Capon in his chapter on "The Generous Ox," "all men should hasten to become very poor or very rich—or both at once, like St. Paul, who had nothing and yet possessed all things."

Both the festal and the ferial are beautiful. Both involve real, skillful cooking and a certain level of creativity on behalf of the chef. What is neither festal nor ferial, meanwhile, is the sort of thing we often find at mid-level chains: food that is eaten in a hurry, food that was prepared without much particular care or interest, food that is neither luxurious nor beautifully understated. In short, food that is only accidentally edible.

You can see where we are going. The mediocrity of Chili's and its ilk is both an assault to the palate and an insult to the art of cuisine, which does not demand expense but does demand attention, time, and creativity. Capon's book is a testament to this notion: the first recipe alone swallows one hundred pages of description, yet a few dollars' worth of ingredients are much the richer for it. A two-for-one special prepared, eaten, and paid for in a matter of forty-five minutes is not *dining*, by this standard, but rather, like the engine at the pump, *refueling*.

O the sad frugality of the middle-income mind. O the humorless neatness of an intellectuality that buys mass-produced candlesticks and carefully puts one at each end of every philosophical mantlepiece! Into the outer darkness with the pill-roller and his wife. They have missed the point of the world; they are purely and simply mad. Man invented cooking before he thought of nutrition. To be sure, food keeps us alive, but that is only its smallest and most temporary work. Its eternal purpose is to furnish our sensibilities against the day when we shall see how gracious the Lord is. Nourishment is necessary only for a while; what we shall need forever is taste.

Savor the thought for a moment. It is good taste that is needed for eternity—an appetite for excellence, which precludes any appetite for what is not. If good taste is what we are after, and not mere sustenance, then work is also required. It is not enough to fill our bellies with anything that is edible any more than we would call "tastefully decorated" a home that was furnished with the exact pieces from the window display. These are easy ways to supply our needs, but they lack the true excellence that is necessary for both the resourceful and creative "stone soups" of the ferial variety and the lavish spreads of the festal type.

Such artistry does not always require expense, or even painstaking difficulty. Earlier, I made the example of the street taco, one of the finest contrivances of God's creation. The components of the best street tacos are simple but extraordinary. Pork: brined and smoked until it falls apart like overripe fruit. Corn tortillas: smoky and just slightly charred. Cheese: tangy. Toppings: fresh. Thanks to global imports, you can make an excellent taco for a couple of dollars per serving, no matter where you live and no matter the time of year. The difference between this and a Chili's plate are those of nuance: time, flavor, care. It is not exceedingly difficult to make a good street taco, but it cannot be done by buying the components premade, and it cannot be done with haste and carelessness for the ingredients. Pork comes to life under a gentle hand, but it turns to death—dry and choking—under the hand of a stern and impatient cook.

There's something distinctly local about this kind of eating: It prizes the family-owned restaurant above the chain establishment and the home chef above them both. This is because the chain restaurant, whatever its creed, cannot offer both artistry and consistency. The Bloomin' Onion has to taste the same wherever you buy it, so the chef retains little or no agency over the food he prepares. While some dishes are good, none can ever be too great for a mediocre hand to execute each night. (And if you think this is selling the cook short, ask yourself if you would sweat through culinary school only to become the head chef at Olive Garden.)

The local restaurant, meanwhile, while not always tasteful, is often so, and it is always unique. The chef may offer you recommendations based on which ingredients are freshest today. He even tailors the dish a bit to your preference, though a good chef is always indisposed to change too much what he presents as his masterpiece. At the local restaurant, you engage the cook on his own merit, rather than on the merit of the corporate chef who designs the national menu. And sometimes, what you find is truly spectacular.

Of course, the home cook is the best of all. Here, you meet the chef face to face. Here, he tells you his inspiration for the meal, or she shyly admits to taking liberties with a family recipe. Here, you know that the food was prepared with care and respect for what it is, what it becomes, and also for *you*, the receiver, who is known and loved by the preparer. It is not a dish that goes out into the darkness and returns empty but one that is eaten at the table alongside its creator, who has offered himself for the feast.

The greatest shame of the mid-level chain restaurant, however, is not that the food is mediocre but that it always tastes the same. The success of big food chains has meant the death of food diversity; while the ingredients come from all over the globe, what we eat is remarkably uniform from chain to chain. Every restaurant serves burgers and Caesar salad. Don't even get me started on kids' menus. Most such restaurants purchase their ingredients from the same bulk food suppliers, too, which means that despite the vast cultural differences between Italy and Mexico, whether prepared as fajitas or in alfredo sauce, the chicken you eat probably came from the same Tyson factory. It is done this way for consistency, for the reliability factor that is a key reason chains are often more popular than the local establishments in small towns. You know what you are getting when you walk into a restaurant with a national reputation. But in exchange for predictability, we have surrendered good foods, both festal and ferial, as well as our good taste. After all, good things are rarely easy to replicate.

Localism

The sad sameness that has made the middle-class chain so popular has snuffed out many mid-level local restaurants, or overpowered them like a heavy-handed chef with the pepper grinder. But good ones do still exist, if we can have the patience to seek them out. And a home cooked meal is always within reach for the man who has friends. These options don't come with two-for-one beers, or loyalty points, or an app, but their dining rooms are full of food that is soulful, and it is created by people whose names you can know. It is in these dining rooms that we discover the sort of good taste which Fr. Capon refers to; the sort of taste that is eternal.

Localism in American Politics

Marco Rubio

In America, the economy has never been a mere tool for amassing financial wealth. Rather, the American economy is a means to realizing American ideas and values: freedom, self-sufficiency, and thriving local communities. Our system values free enterprise insofar as it meets the needs of American citizens and families. Our system, in other words, is one of common-good capitalism.

Pursuing the common good should be common sense. Unfortunately, in our day, it isn't. For the past two decades, leading American policymakers and businessmen have opted not for common-good capitalism but for big-government socialism or free-market fundamentalism. These flawed systems stand opposed to the United States' true economic heritage.

Among other failures, both socialism and free-market fundamentalism foster disdain for the role of local communities. Big-government socialism takes from local communities the ability to solve their own problems, and it overrides them with mandates (usually socially leftist ones) from Washington, D.C. Free-market fundamentalism, on the other hand, undermines small businesses and rationalizes off-shoring jobs to other countries.

Localism

Proponents of these systems argue they are necessary for achieving progress and growth for the country as a whole. They're missing the fact that national progress and growth ring hollow without strong local communities. G. K. Chesterton understood this idea when he wrote, "The way to make a living thing is to make it local." In other words, human beings flourish (or fail) at the level of their families, small businesses, and towns. More than anything else, it is in these institutions and networks of relationships that the average person finds meaning, dignity, and the strength to build a better life.

If this was true for Chesterton's England, it is truer of the United States. Local communities have formed the beating heart of our Republic since the Founding. When Alexis de Tocqueville visited America in the nineteenth century, he found the New England townships an essential support to the new system of self-government. In his own words: "Town meetings are to liberty what primary schools are to science; they bring it within the people's reach, they teach men how to use and how to enjoy it. A nation may establish a free government, but without municipal institutions, it cannot have the spirit of liberty."

The Founders themselves were just as aware of the vital importance of local communities. The Founding Father James Wilson said that the family, the most basic local institution, is the "true origin of society." And it was to safeguard local communities that the framers of the Constitution established the system of federalism, under which the relative autonomy of states and municipalities was protected from the centralizing influence of the national government.

Federalism is in many ways the Catholic Social Teaching principle of subsidiarity enacted in law. In the encyclical *Quadragesimo Anno*, Pope Pius XI writes that it is "a grave evil and disturbance of right order to assign to a greater and higher association what lesser and subordinate organizations can do." This is the logic of subsidiarity. According to Pius, the closer decisions are made to those most directly affected by them, the better. Like Pius and his predecessor Leo XIII, early American leaders recognized the primacy of the local community.

Protecting and supporting local communities remained a priority for policymakers throughout most of the United States' history. In the years of the early Republic, statesmen such as Alexander Hamilton and Henry Clay crafted national policies that encouraged the development of local manufacturing. Up through the mid-twentieth century, it was the consensus view that the federal government has a constructive role to play in providing an economic structure beneficial to states and municipalities—in which working Americans can find dignified jobs, raise families with a reasonable standard of living, and build community with their neighbors.

However, toward the end of the Cold War, American politicians and businessmen forged a new, bipartisan economic consensus, one of free-market fundamentalism. Convinced it was laissez-faire policies that enabled the United States to beat the Soviet Union, elites from Bill Clinton to Bill Gates embraced an ideology that enshrined efficiency as the greatest economic value, the Gross Domestic Product as the highest standard of national prosperity, and free trade as an unqualified good. That ideology still reigns supreme in leading institutions throughout the country.

Free-market fundamentalism is based on the assumption that people are shoppers above all else and that lower prices for consumer goods are more valuable than productive capacity, dignified work, and community viability. But that assumption is false. People are not just shoppers, they are also spouses, parents, siblings, and workers. If they are to lead flourishing lives, they need productive industries, dignified jobs, and viable communities far more than they need low prices.

The pursuit of unqualified trade has enriched nationless corporations, which have been able to cut costs by moving their factories to countries that employ slave labor, such as Communist China. Moreover, it has boosted the stock market, providing an illusion of wealth. However, these gains have been at the expense of ordinary Americans, whose jobs have been lost to foreign workers and whose small businesses (vital local institutions) have been replaced by Amazon delivery services and big-box stores.

We see the tragic results across the country, but particularly in regions that once relied on domestic industry for community life. Thousands of our small towns and manufacturing centers are now characterized by historic lows of male labor force participation, marriage, and breadwinning capacity on the one hand, and historic highs of drug addiction, social isolation, and suicide on the other.

Free-market fundamentalists argue that the bipartisan economic consensus frees private enterprise from overbearing government regulations. In reality, though, Washington's power grows as the local community's decreases. The quest for totally free trade entails the destruction of local forms of economic regulation and authority. It does not actually enhance individual choice. Instead, it leaves individuals at the mercy of mega-corporations such as Amazon—as well as foreign powers like Communist China, which provides those corporations with production workers and oversees their factories. And as the sociologist Robert Nisbet observed, the growth of corporations prompts the expansion of the only remaining regulatory power, the federal government, to contain them.

This paradoxical relationship explains how top-down government programs have expanded side-by-side with America's mega-corporations over the past few decades. Progressives see Americans' wages are insufficient, and they recognize that big business is often part of the problem. But rather than use the government to strengthen local communities, their response is to give Washington control over everyday details of American life and drag our country deeper into debt.

This is simply a proposal for socialism, and it would do nothing to help ordinary citizens. In fact, labyrinthine regulations and bureaucratic programs favor large corporations with teams of legal experts far more than workers and small businesses. Chesterton was right when he quipped that "Big Business and State Socialism are very much alike."

The key to renewing America's prosperity is neither pursuing unqualified free trade nor embracing the welfare state but rather recommitting ourselves to the advancement of local communities through common-sense public policy. For too long, we have chosen economic efficiency and administrative bureaucracy over stable jobs that provide the basis for flourishing families and towns. Today, laws that strengthen domestic industry and support community institutions such as small businesses could do much to restore American Main Street.

Industrial policy is a dirty term for market ideologues, but it has been a core element of the American tradition for the majority of our country's history. In the Founding era, Hamilton proposed supporting domestic manufacturing through targeted subsidies. Later, Henry Clay commended infrastructure projects that would facilitate private enterprise. In the twentieth century, it was robust industrial policy that enabled the United States to defeat the combined might of Imperial Japan and Nazi Germany.

Localism

A renewed industrial policy would make the United States less dependent on foreign producers like Communist China, which wields far more power over our corporations than a totalitarian, genocidal regime ever should. It would also bring back more stable, dignified jobs to American workers from overseas.

Supporting domestic industry is not just about helping big manufacturing companies, either. When our economy faltered during the initial COVID-19 lockdowns, I worked with my colleagues in the U.S. Small Business Administration to create the Paycheck Protection Program (PPP), which became law in March 2020. The PPP funneled more than $800 billion into American small businesses, giving them the resources they needed to keep their doors open and their employees on payroll. It was so successful that economist Doug Holtz-Eakin called it "the single most effective fiscal policy ever undertaken by the United States government." The PPP is proof that, in a moment of crisis, Washington can protect small businesses without absorbing or replacing them.

Other straightforward ways the government can advance and help revitalize American local communities include federal tax reforms. Currently, the U.S. tax code rewards companies for spending their capital on stock buybacks, instead of physical investment in the economy. We should change this incentive to encourage reinvestment of profits into innovation and business development.

The tax code can also be reformed to strengthen families. In 2017, Senator Mike Lee (R-UT) and I successfully doubled the federal child tax credit, allowing breadwinners to keep more of their pay. Millions of families across the income spectrum benefited. Policies such as these discourage the speculative finance-capitalism that Pope Benedict XVI criticized, and they reward genuine productivity when wages are insufficient. They help hard-working

Americans in their efforts to raise families, acquire property, and build communities.

A return to common sense and the pursuit of the common good is a vision for the United States' future that Abraham Lincoln—who described his ideal economy as a network of small businesses free from "crowned-kings, money-kings, and land-kings" alike—would be proud of. It is also a vision that should sit well with Chestertonian localists.

Chesterton dreamed of a world in which every man could own property, produce authentically valuable goods, and support a family on his own resources. Reaching for that world is the true American tradition, and we have almost lost it. The federal government can only do so much to remedy the problem, but what it can do, it should.

A Local Triumph in Italy

Marco Sermarini

So distributism—I'll make it very short and very simple, don't be afraid—What was the argument of Belloc and Chesterton and all these other nutters who were talking about how to make society a little more beautiful and a little more livable? Let's say that at the essence, at the basis of civilized living, there must be three things. At the basis of social life there has to be labor, land (because they were mainly talking about those who came from the peasantry) and capital (which does not have to be the capital that we mean now, but what someone keeps aside and what has to be used to sustain life).

When these three elements do not belong to the majority of the people living who live in a society, then it is a state basically leading to serfdom—so much so that Belloc wrote an important, interesting, intelligent, extraordinary book called *The Servile State*, which explains just what servitude and slavery consists of. And then these guys from San Benedetto del Tronto—who you may not know and who have a madman at their head—what did they do? They have done an extraordinary thing. They have set up a school—I don't know if you know it, it's called "Chesterton"—that applies this concept of distributism literally because they have soil (i.e. the kids that attend it).

The capital consists of what? It consists of their culture, knowledge of their life and faith. Then by holding all these things together here, they have created something beautiful and extraordinary that is meant to live and survive, and so we are also here to support them in this thing.

In June 2010, my journalist friend Alessandro Gnocchi spoke these words during the Eighth Annual Chesterton Day, an event we host in San Benedetto del Tronto, Italy. I found his words brilliant since they summarized very important concepts in a few lines and recognized something new, linking it with tradition and distributism. The work we had been doing for about two years at the time was indeed a distributist achievement.

The late Stratford Caldecott in June 2012 spoke at the Tenth Chesterton Day and among other things told us:

I agree that society today is highly developed and highly complex, so the mechanism itself is difficult to change.... For example, I have a friend in Sierra Leone [John Kanu, director of the Sierra Leone Chesterton Center] in Africa, who came to Oxford and studied Chesterton and realized that these ideas could be used in his country, one of the poorest in the world.... So he founded this "Chesterton Society" to teach people the importance of farming and animal husbandry. This is a way to satisfy their humanity, to benefit society. So they partner up, they buy the land and use it and make arrangements with the local chiefs, then they buy the equipment and train people to use this equipment. So it's like a "community school," and they have a football club to involve young people and to give a sense of partnership....

Our economic system is not working well anymore and I think the crisis is not over yet. Many people are now going back to distributism to develop new forms of economic thinking.

Living experiences have a lot to teach us. This "empirical" approach definitely outweighs all calculations, systems, and equations of an economic nature, and it addresses the common objection about the impossibility of changing the course of today's society. The standard view is that if an idea proposing to change the economic aspect of life is to be taken seriously, it must be reducible to equations or systems or models. And it must be repeatable. In other words, without the chrisms of formal economics, an idea would have no hope of development. But this impression is not true. Distributism can be achieved because it corresponds to human hearts, and if there are formulas or models to summarize it, these follow concrete experiences, made up of names, faces, and stories. There are past experiences that teach us life prevails over theory. Two examples are the Italian *Monti di Pietà* and the Jesuit *reducciones* in Paraguay.

But we have seen what has happened in our town of San Benedetto del Tronto, that distributism is not a dream but a reality, a necessary way to save ourselves from the servile state. Our story needs some more elaboration. In July 2008, my family, along with a few others, decided to give continuity to the Catholic educational experience born first at home by taking advantage of a principle laid down in the Italian Constitution that allows parents to educate and instruct their children at home according to their own convictions. Abroad this practice is called homeschooling, and it's an everyday thing; but here we are regarded like Martians. We also decided to homeschool our children all together and to extend this possibility to other families as well. In September of that same year, we opened the (metaphorical) doors of our new school. Our motto: "A dead thing can go with the stream, but only a living thing can go against it." And this immortal line of Chesterton's was supplemented by two more points from his pen:

> People are inundated, blinded, deafened, and mentally paralyzed by a flood of vulgar and tasteless externals, leaving them no time for leisure, thought, or creation from within themselves.

And:

> To make a long story short, the evil I am trying to warn you of is not excessive democracy, it is not excessive ugliness, it is not excessive anarchy. It might be stated thus: it is standardization by a low standard.

Here I return to Stratford Caldecott:

> Distributism is the view that private property should be distributed widely in society rather than being concentrated in a few hands. And this is aimed at making it possible for more and more people to be able to be responsible for their families through productive and worthy work.... The basis of the movement was the importance of families against this idea of capitalism concentrating wealth in a few hands.

Our school relies on those who make it (teachers, parents, and pupils) as well as the support of those who esteem it. Fundamentally, it is the expression of a people. Very low tuition fees are flanked by a system of fundraising. A group of people freely pay a weekly fee by giving what they can to support our work and keep it financially stable. Each man actually supports the ground on

which he himself rests his feet, the cordial and concrete relationships on which he bases his life. The friendly faces that form the
cells of our organism are the future of a good way of life because
without Christian education and Christian life, there is no future.
Our banner is that of Monti di Pietà, an ancient and glorious
institution whose main architects were the Franciscans, men of
the stature of St. Bernardine of Siena and St. James della Marca,
my fellow countryman.

In our school, we have built a different independent entity, an
absolutely revolutionary method that sets aside:

❖ The anti-Catholic idea that schooling can only be done by
the state, which does not correspond to the way schooling
originated in Western Europe, namely from the institutions that formed our way of life—monasteries, cathedrals,
fraternities, and guilds;

❖ The capitalist banking system, considered to be the only
source of credit. For centuries our civilization used different methods for credit, but they are now forgotten.
Capitalism is based on the accumulation of money, distributism on its dissemination, as well as a popular, familial commitment to thrift;

❖ The idea that one should organize one's life and that of
one's family according to patterns not our own that are
often far from one's own ideals. Conformism is the real
challenge against the establishment of the distributist state.
We have to think about life differently than the way the
stifling powers that be imposed on us. Education is the
tool that can give us hope.

Moreover, founding the school brought home to us the reality that making some choices calls into question others: if I can
make a school, if I plan to support it, and if in order to support

the school I have decided to allocate a more or less considerable part of my savings, then this means that:

* ❖ My savings may have an unconventional destination (they may not end up in banks, which support a system opposite to the one we build);
* ❖ The purpose of savings can also be to build a different world; man does not express himself by consuming but by building;
* ❖ I can decide to work to build this world, like the Benedictine monks one thousand five hundred years ago. The real revolution of Benedictine monasticism was neither economic nor technological but was *nihil amori Christi praeponere* — "to prefer nothing above the love of Christ."

As G. K. Chesterton says in "The Flag of the World":

> For our titanic purposes of faith and revolution, what we need is not the cold acceptance of the world as a compromise, but some way in which we can heartily hate and heartily love it. We do not want joy and anger to neutralize each other and produce a surly contentment; we want a fiercer delight and a fiercer discontent. We have to feel the universe at once as an ogre's castle, to be stormed, and yet as our own cottage, to which we can return at evening.

Eventually, our group was able to purchase land and a house in a beautiful place overlooking our town on the hill of Santa Lucia. Normally, such an enterprise would have necessitated our group applying for a bank loan and using bank credit, but we decided to buy the house on the hill by subscribing to an increase in the cooperative's capital stock and by collecting members' savings. Each member provided his or her own resources — financial but also professional — for the renovation of the first house and the construction of a second one, working for free as volunteer members of the cooperative, offering his or her professional work for free, or advocating deals for lower prices and much more. The house now belongs to each and every member, to the people who willed the school to happen. The members help each other concretely and do not depend on the benevolence of a bank that goes about its business and does not care about *our* "business." We are free.

The cooperative that runs the school administers many of the activities of our *Opera G. K. Chesterton*: a sports club, an after-school club, a buying group for basic necessities, an enterprise to put disadvantaged people back to work, organized construction work, agricultural work, a vegetable garden, a silk-screen printing shop, and more. This localized cooperation creates a different idea of "welfare" based on education, which is the engine of any healthy society or culture. Time for leisure, contemplation, and imagination provides for a spectacular expression of a people's creativity and genius. It grows friendly and loving relationships, the sharing of one's family time, the future of one's society—our school is like a little kingdom made up of many little kingdoms of common sense, all of which provide us a safe haven from the morbid individualism, materialism, and consumerism of capitalism.

Our school is a local project, but even the locals don't yet get it. On a building in my town, for example, some anarchist spray-painted the words "produce, consume, and die." Unfortunately, he knows neither distributism nor us.

What is happening on Santa Lucia Hill in San Benedetto del Tronto is what Chesterton and Belloc would refer to as the "Distributist State," the weaving of small family republics; the family is the real flywheel of everything, and it is that small republic on which everything depends.

I want to go further. Such a system is based on the idea of the irreplaceability of mutual help. As Stratford Caldecott said, "Distributism is less impractical than is often supposed—though it depends, as I say later, on the presence of a certain spirit of cooperation. In less developed countries it is eminently practical, and even in the developed West it may suggest viable alternatives to an economic system arguably on the verge of collapse." Some of these alternative approaches to business and banking are mentioned in the encyclical *Caritas in Veritate* by Pope Benedict XVI.

Christian charity has no set limits on what can be implemented. We have already mentioned The Sierra Leone Chesterton Center founded by John Kanu, who also contributed to this volume. We have friends in Norcia, the monks of the local Benedictine monastery, too; they live in a similar way, brewing their beer in the monastery and living as a group of men building a world in which nothing is put before the love of Christ. A society made up of "republics" like these, welded together by bonds of mutual help founded in Our Lord Jesus Christ, can establish a network of good and humane relationships for a truer life and can create a valid and useful fabric to weather any storm. I do not think I am venturing to compare these albeit humble experiences with the yearning for Truth that moved St. Benedict of Norcia centuries ago.

Nihil amori Christi praeponere.

Localism: The Context for
Catholic Social Teaching

Thomas Storck

What is localism, and what does it have to do with Catholic Social Teaching? Is localism merely a nostalgia for a past and a way of life that, however good it may have been, is now lost and cannot be recovered? If so, what does the Church's social thought have to do with it? The renewal of Catholic social doctrine, beginning with Leo XIII and extending to the present pontificate, always has spoken to the times we actually live in, not to a past that cannot be recreated. It has never been an exercise in nostalgic longing.

The picture, however, is not as simple as the foregoing might suggest. For while they have always been realists, the supreme pontiffs have never hesitated to take the good things that existed in the past and urge that they be recreated, in some form, in the present. Pope Pius XI made this very clear when speaking of the medieval economic order in his encyclical *Quadragesimo Anno*:

> At one period there existed a social order which, though by no means perfect in every respect, corresponded nevertheless in a certain measure to right reason according to the needs and conditions of the times. That this order has long

since perished is not due to the fact that it was incapable of development and adaptation to changing needs and circumstances, but rather to the wrong-doing of men. Men were hardened in excessive self-love and refused to extend that order, as was their duty, to the increasing numbers of the people; or else, deceived by the attractions of false liberty and other errors, they grew impatient of every restraint and endeavored to throw off all authority. (no. 97)

So just as Pius XI here praises the essential notes of the medieval social order and economy, while recognizing the need to develop and adapt them, we can say the same about localism. It need not be merely a longing for a vanished way of life, but something dynamic and always relevant. But what exactly is it; what can the term reasonably mean?

Though like any other broad term in socio-political discourse, such as conservatism or liberalism, localism doubtless means different things to different people, I think it is possible to formulate an understanding that is both accurate and true to the intentions of most of those who employ it. I would call "localism," then, an attitude: an attitude that recognizes that just as human beings are necessarily rooted in particular times, so we are rooted in particular places. And without this rootedness, we are not complete as human persons; we lack an essential dimension, namely, our natural relations with others. For unless we recognize that we are neither isolated atoms nor beings whose interactions with our fellows are to be dictated merely by convenience and self-interest, we will not truly comprehend human nature.

If, however, we understand that we are necessarily parts of a community of persons with whom we have bonds, more or less natural, of numerous kinds, we will see that it is only as members of families, parishes, neighborhoods, workplaces, fraternal groups, municipalities, and so on, that we can fully realize our personhood and humanity. In *Caritas in Veritate*, Benedict XVI wrote of our need for personal relations that go beyond those dictated by either the imperatives of politics or the market:

> When both the logic of the market and the logic of the State come to an agreement that each will continue to exercise a monopoly over its respective area of influence, in the long term much is lost: solidarity in relations between citizens, participation and adherence, actions of gratuitousness, all of which stand in contrast with *giving in order to acquire* (the logic of exchange) and *giving through duty* (the logic of public obligation, imposed by State law). (no. 39)

Of course, localism does not mean that we are nothing more than creatures of a particular locale, that we ought simply to accept all the ideas or viewpoints, bad as well as good, that characterize our own place or time. In fact, part of becoming a *Catholic*, a member of the universal Church intended for all of mankind, is to overcome the prejudices and limited outlooks that every place and time is subject to. Like any other characteristic or feature of life on earth, localist impulses must be governed by the gospel.

In the same encyclical of Pius XI that I quoted above, the pontiff spoke of "the highly developed social life which once flourished in a variety of prosperous and interdependent institutions," but that, as he goes on to say, "has been damaged and all but ruined." Such a "highly developed social life" was, of course, local, not only because of the state of technology existing at the time, but more fundamentally because only at the local level can such a social life be truly based on genuine human interactions. And if we hope once again to be able to participate in such a "highly developed social life," we must reexamine our attitudes toward the local and, instead of scorning it as something necessarily "provincial" or "small-townish," discern in it one of the fundamental principles of a happy social order.

But in what exactly did this "highly developed social life" consist? Was it more than merely a friendly attitude toward one's neighbors and fellow townsmen? To understand what Pope Pius XI was primarily referring to here, let us probe some specifics of papal proposals for the social order. Looking again at *Quadragesimo Anno*, immediately after the passage I just quoted, the pope laments the fact that the ruin of this intricate social order has left "virtually only individuals and the State, with no little harm to the latter. [For] the State, deprived of a supporting social structure, and now encumbered with all the burdens once borne by the disbanded associations, is in consequence overwhelmed and submerged by endless affairs and responsibilities" (no. 78).

We see here one of the key principles of Catholic social doctrine. While the Church by no means regards the state as an evil, not even as a necessary evil, and while she gives ample scope and honor to the state's duties and functions, she likewise does not regard the civil authority as the immediate and sole source for addressing all questions that arise in the life of a nation or people. That is why in the very next section Pius enunciates the famous principle of subsidiarity, according to which "it is an injustice and at the same time a grave evil and a disturbance of right order, to transfer to the larger and higher collectivity functions which can be performed and provided for by lesser and subordinate bodies."

The state certainly has responsibilities in the social order, but by and large the immediate and direct responsibility rests with other bodies, bodies that ideally should be part of that "highly developed social life" that unfortunately has pretty much disappeared, while the state's primary role in such matters consists in making sure that the lower bodies are in fact functioning as they should, or as Pius XI put it, "directing, supervising, encouraging, restraining, as circumstances suggest or necessity demands" (no. 80).

But what are these "lesser and subordinate bodies," and what do they have to do with localism? Contrary to the notions of some, the pope was not referring to private, voluntary organizations, still less to businesses and other for-profit entities. One of the key themes of *Quadragesimo Anno*, and one that is by no means absent from the social teaching of later pontiffs, was the need to reestablish some modern version of the medieval guilds.

Lest the reader react with a sigh and consign me to those hopelessly addicted to a romantic medievalism, let me explain. The guild principle is not something that merely characterized the economies of medieval cities but is something that has an enduring relevance. When we look at the tedious and endless squabbles in this country between those who style themselves conservatives and those who call themselves liberals, I think we may be able to discern why this is so. Liberals have tended to recognize the many injustices that arise in the economy—injustices involving wages, working conditions, product quality, prices, and so on. And their response to these undoubted injustices has usually been to establish a new government agency to address the problem. Sometimes, no doubt, this *was* the correct response.

But sometimes, also, the conservatives were right to point out that the state was becoming too big, was assuming responsibilities for which it was not fitted, was attempting a one-size-fits-all approach to problems that in fact differed from locality to locality. Americans, however—saddled as we are with the unfortunate legacy of John Locke's philosophy of government—generally knew no way out of the dilemma of too little government or too much government. Seldom did it occur to anyone that perhaps there was another and better way.

This other and better way was precisely that of the guild principle, namely the immediate and normal regulation of workplace issues by groups composed of both workers and managers and owners and, as appropriate, by consumer groups as well. Such groups would give real power to all involved and are not to be understood as the company unions of the past, usually mere tools of management in which workers had little or no real voice. Modern guilds, or occupational groups as they are better termed, would be institutions with real authority, whose guiding principle would be the subordination of the wishes of both labor and owners to the demands of justice and the health of the industry and overall economy.

Now at this point it is probably true that the reestablishment of something such as guilds on a large scale is an impossibility. But why is this? Why does it seem like a hopeless task? In great measure because we have lost the attitude that I have termed localism. Corporations today are nationwide, even global. As we witnessed recently, our supply chains originate in many places throughout the world and involve all sorts of entities, corporations, holding companies, and the like.

To unravel all of this would be a daunting task. But all this superstructure was built up because in the first place Americans, and moderns in general, turned away from the idea that it was healthier if we were rooted in a place than if we assumed the role of free-floating social atoms that modernity was all too eager to assign to us. A healthy and just economy cannot be built upon a diseased social order. Not every economic organization of society is susceptible of being healed. A cancer cannot be turned into healthy cells; it can only be killed or excised. Occupational groups will not work well in an economy dominated by transnational corporations. They require some local sense if they are to function well, for the problems they address are always concrete and immediate.

So what works well in one place might not work well in another, what is a living wage in one place is far from adequate in another; Workplace culture, technology, the legal structure—all these differ substantially from one nation to another, and often even within a particular nation. Any institution created to address economic and industrial issues must be locally focused to be effective. Of course, this does not mean that there are not larger issues that such groups must attend to, but only if they have a healthy local setting in the first place.

Let us look at another example: health care. Already in another of his encyclicals, *Casti Connubii*, Pius XI had indicated the state's necessary role in ensuring adequate health care for its citizens (see nos. 118, 120, 121). But how is this to be done? By a centralized government agency? While this can be acceptable in lieu of a feasible alternative, I do not think it is the best way.

That better way is suggested again by Pope Pius when, addressing the economic needs of families, he speaks of "joint aid by private or public guilds," with a footnote referring back to Leo XIII's *Rerum Novarum*. In this latter document, Pope Leo had spoken of societies akin to guilds, one of whose objects was providing mutual support and aid to its members. It is easy to imagine a widespread network of such mutual aid societies or cooperatives organized with the intention of providing health care to their members. Such associations actually existed in the late nineteenth and early twentieth century United States, often sponsored by fraternal societies.

Undoubtedly, these societies would require state support and regulation of some kind, at the least some kind of tax exemption, but they would not be state agencies. The point here, however, is that such societies pretty much depend on localism for their successful existence. Probably the chief reason why this idea would seem impractical today is because of our excessive mobility. Moving about in pursuit of jobs, education, and other reasons is pretty much the norm. It would be hard to organize and successfully maintain a mutual aid society or cooperative if its membership were continually changing.

Both the logic of the market and the logic of the modern state effectively disregard the idea of place. Place means nothing in a capitalist economy, which seeks both workers and raw materials anywhere it can find them—wherever they can be obtained most cheaply. Likewise, place is not important to the modern state, which insists on treating its citizens as so many isolated atoms in a void and thereby proclaims that cultural groupings are of no importance, indeed, are inimical to its understanding of democracy. Localism is counter to both of these; indeed, it is counter to the chief assumptions upon which modernity has been built. But some kind of localism must be our goal if we are to have any success in creating a happier and more just society.

There is one more item that I think must be brought up by anyone attempting an honest defense of localism. To many people, the idea of staying in one's place, in the place of our birth or at least where we have significant natural attachments, is, frankly, limiting, boring, even stultifying. One might recall the line from the World War I era song, "How ya gonna keep 'em down on the farm, after they've seen Paree?" Any defense of localism that fails to acknowledge a certain truth to this charge will be inadequate.

For it is a fact that American farm life and small-town life, such as many experienced it in the nineteenth century and even till today, was often limited and isolated. But it was so not because it was local or even rural but because of the way we had structured that kind of life. Life on free-standing farmsteads, for example, did inhibit the formation of rich cultures, such as are associated with traditional rural life in Europe or Mexico and elsewhere, where farming families lived in or near villages and farmed the surrounding lands. But small-town America was often limited in its cultural or economic opportunities. The reason for this limitation, though, was the pressure of our mass commercial civilization that did so much to destroy distinct local cultures and imposed a standardized way of life that people tried to escape by moving to big cities. Yet there is no reason that rural areas need to be boring or limiting. In Europe, even today, there is less felt need to leave one's locale for a better life, and, as a consequence, many university students are content to live at home and attend nearby institutions.

This kind of life requires an attitude toward place and land often lacking in our history. In his book *It All Turns on Affection*, Wendell Berry (quoting from Wallace Stegner) says that the settlers of North America have been largely "boomers" rather than "stickers":

> Boomers are "those who pillage and run," who want "to make a killing and end up on Easy Street," whereas stickers are "those who settle, and love the life they have made and the place they have made it in." "Boomer" names a kind of person and ambition that is the major theme, so far, of the history of the European races in our country. "Sticker" names a kind of person and desire that is, so far, a minor theme of that history.

Localism

A local culture cannot be built by boomers; it can be built only by those who are willing to stay in a place and work to create a society worthy of human beings, one that prevents material things and especially money from being seen as the chief social good. There is no reason why people must move about to find satisfying lives, both economically and culturally. If we can be freed from our crazed addiction to overexcitement, then we can realize a fulfilling existence without continual moving about. But we must be willing to help build local institutions, create local cultures, without which many people will look at the places they left behind and say, "Good riddance!"

In his seminal work *Religion and the Rise of Western Culture*, the Catholic historian Christopher Dawson wrote:

> Thus the medieval city was a community of communities in which the same principles of corporate rights and chartered liberties applied equally to the whole and to the parts. For the medieval idea of liberty, which finds it highest expression in the life of the free cities, was not the right of the individual to follow his own will, but the privilege of sharing in a highly organized form of corporate life which possessed its own constitution and rights of self-government. In many cases this constitution was hierarchical and authoritarian, but as every corporation had its own rights in the life of the city, so every individual had his place and his rights in the life of the gild.

If we are ever to achieve something like a culture oriented to the principle of localism, then we must first achieve an attitude akin to what Dawson describes here, a joy in participating in the "highly organized form of corporate life," in "the highly developed social life which once flourished in a variety of prosperous and interdependent institutions," as Pope Pius XI put it. These can exist only if we adopt the attitude that place is worth something, worth knowing, even worth loving. *That* is the first requirement of localism: to know and to love our place. It is not impossible if enough of us want it.

The Whole Creation

Michael Dominic Taylor

Christ was born into a world that had been prepared for His arrival, knowingly or not, from the very start. Paul reported to the Romans that, "Ever since the creation of the world his invisible nature, namely, his eternal power and deity, has been clearly perceived in the things that have been made" (Rom. 1:20). Discerning Hebrews and wise men could read the scriptures and the stars, Virgil reports a prophecy of the Cumaean Sibyl, and the temple to an unknown god awaited Paul in Athens. Nevertheless, as Christ forewarned, the Sanhedrin would reject Him, the powerful of the world would reject His gospel, and His followers would be persecuted.

Just as Christ's miracles grew in strength as His public ministry progressed toward His Passion, Christ's instructions to His disciples would broaden in scale and scope: first He sent them only to "the lost sheep of the house of Israel" (Matt. 10:6), then, shortly before His Passion, to "all the nations" (Matt. 24:14) and then to "the whole world" (Matt. 26:13), until finally, after His Resurrection, in Christ's final commission before His Ascension, He told His disciples: "Go into all the world and proclaim the good news to the whole creation" (Mark 16:15).

Localism

It would be easy to overlook the difference between "all nations" and "the whole creation," yet to do so would be to overlook the cosmic dimension of the Christian gospel, and it would limit Christ's mission to an exclusively human drama set against a wholly natural and neutral backdrop with no ultimate significance. However, this seemingly benign demarcation undermines the very logic of Ceation and the meaning of the human community.

I. Wise Pagans and Christian Community

The first Christians would be those who stepped out from among the children of Israel and the pagans of the Greco-Roman world. The notions of the Greek *polis* and Roman *civitas* contained innate wisdom about the mutual dependence of all men. Roman peoples, accustomed to divinizing their heroes and to seeing themselves as heirs to the eternal glory of Rome, were not unprepared to accept the Communion of the Saints and the Church as the Body of Christ. Atomists aside, virtually all ancient people perceived a natural moral order and believed in the immortality of the soul. Truly, the harvest was great, but the laborers were few (see Matt. 9:37).

Of course, a great deal of purification was also needed. As G. K. Chesterton observed in his study of St. Francis of Assisi, by walking "the high road of reason and nature," pagan nature-worship always seemed to end up mired in the worship of the unnatural. Paganism could not avoid this downfall because it could not account for Original Sin. In this sense, the good news of Christ's victory over Original Sin was almost on a par with the good news of Original Sin itself!

Christianity, with its dimensions of penitence and austerity, would bring to the West that purification it sorely needed. Thanks in large part to St. Benedict, western monasticism, with its evangelical counsels of chastity, poverty, and obedience, educated and civilized a huge area of the world. In the end, Chesterton concludes, "the pagans were wiser than paganism; that is why the pagans became Christians."

This purification was not a puritanical asceticism but one inspired with the overflowing love of the Trinity and filled with joyful gratitude. Responding to the accusation that the feasts and festivals of Christianity were of pagan origin, Chesterton replied: "they might as well say that our legs are of pagan origin.... One of the chief claims of Christian civilization is to have preserved things of pagan origin. In short, in the old religious countries men continue to dance; while in the new scientific cities they are often content to drudge."

It must be pointed out that between "old religion" and the building of the "scientific cities" there were a number of crucial modern developments. When Aquinas's great synthesis of the best of pagan philosophy into a fully Christian worldview was outlawed in 1277 by the bishop of Paris, along with other dangerous ideas, the philosophical vacuum would give rise to Scotus's "univocity of being" and Ockham's nominalism. These wayward philosophies would set the stage for materialism, rationalism, and voluntarism with their disdain for the word and the bifurcation of the intellect and the will.

By the time Aquinas's work was vindicated in 1325, the damage had already been done. While Aquinas's work would be incorporated into the *via antica* of theological training, the so-called *via moderna* based in the work of Scotus and Ockham had already taken shape. It was this latter in which Luther and many of his contemporaries would be educated and that effectively severed the relationship between philosophy and theology. The burgeoning European cities, enriched through trade and technical innovation, would grow as economic centers, leading the way toward the new, empirical, scientific age.

As it would turn out, Christianity was now facing something far graver than the quaint pagans of old. In fact, it would become clear that what the wise pagans and the Christians shared was a reverence for the spiritual dimension of the world. This was the realization of Charles Péguy when he said that "one can make a Christian from a pagan soul, but not from a man with no soul." C. S. Lewis too sensed the loss of our common inheritance. As he wrote in a letter to his friend St. Giovanni Calabria, "Moral relativity is the enemy we have to overcome before we tackle Atheism. I would almost dare to say 'First let us make the younger generation good pagans and afterwards let us make them Christians.'"

Modernity hadn't done away with Christianity, but it had undermined it greatly by definitively banishing what was best in paganism. Nature-worship was most certainly something to be overcome: St. Boniface, the eighth-century missionary to the Germans, gave us a clear image of that when he chopped down the oak tree that was worshipped by the local pagans. But it seems that since the dawn of the modern age and the building of the first scientific city, something inherently human has also been undermined, often leaving the name and trappings of Christianity intact while crippling its soul.

II. The Ontological Foundations of Community

The fundamental intuitions of the Greek *polis* and Roman *civitas* had little to do with the Hobbesian fear of one's fellow man. Modern man and modern society are founded on the theory of the atomistic and autonomous man who can only relate to others extrinsically through contractual relationships. The modern scientific city is a fully contractual city in which any remnant of covenant has been stripped from civil life. But it was not always this way.

To appreciate what a Christian community should be, we must first ask what a truly human community is, for grace builds on nature. What sets the human person apart is his ability to enter into full communion with God, which is the fulfillment of what it means to be a creature created by God *ex nihilo*. The synthesis of Thomas Aquinas is bound together by this fundamental recognition: everything that exists is *creatura*. In his book *The Silence of St. Thomas*, Josef Pieper argued that the notion of Creation—a notion he felt was woefully neglected—"determines and characterizes the interior structure of *nearly all* the basic concepts in St. Thomas's philosophy of Being." Created Being is no neutral backdrop, simply there; all being is created, and the goodness, truth, and beauty of created things are not accidental properties but "synonyms for 'existing.'"

Here it is essential to recall that existence is an act—the *actus essendi*—that defines the present in which we live and move precisely *as present*. In short, Thomas taught that a creature is being created in each instant and is simultaneously the recipient of both his existence and his essence, along with the constitutive relations these imply. The creatures of this world do not first "possess themselves" and only then enter into relation with others after the fact. Rather, receptivity and relationality are inscribed into the original gift of being that is ontologically prior not only to self-communication through action, but even to *self-possession*.

This is the crucial point: relationality is essential to who one is, and it plays a decisive role in forming the individual. This was what then-Cardinal Ratzinger was referring to when he said that "*relatio* stands beside substance as an equally primordial form of being." One cannot be understood without the other. *Being* and *action* mutually imply each other in a duality-within-unity in which *being* is prior. To build community, then, is to act upon that which has already been received, in such a way as to correspond to the reality of the gift of Creation.

III. In the World and of the World

Thus, community is not "built" but given, and it must be received and responded to in turn. And because the people around us, but also the animals, vegetables, minerals, and the land we inhabit, are true creatures, loved by God in their unique individuality, we are bound to them and owe them a response. What I would like to suggest here is that the most concrete foundation of *communitas* given to us, the common ground we share as communities, may very well be *the ground beneath our feet*.

This truth was undermined by modernity both intellectually—flattening the natural into a uniform backdrop of mechanistic indifference—and technologically—by making us increasingly independent from the land and from each other. Local culture and love of place has resisted this trend, but the inexorable laws of the economy of scale never cease to bring forth new affronts to our sense of place and propriety.

For the majority of human communities, commitment to and affection for the place where one lived was simply natural. The first "intentional communities" were monastic. But it was not incidental that these communities set down the deepest of roots wherever they arrived, binding their commitment to God with a commitment to place and community by a solemn vow of stability. In imitation of St. Benedict, monks and nuns abandoned the world of urban wickedness for the world of Creation.

Aquinas points out that "the world" has three meanings in Scripture, the first two referring to Creation: the original Creation of God and Creation perfected in Christ. It's only the third that refers to what Tolkien would call the "twisting" of Creation into something perverse. It is to this that John refers when he says, "the whole world lies under the power of the evil one" (1 John 5:19). The world itself is good, true, and beautiful by its very existence. The Catholic tradition, only by attending to the truth of Creation in its commitment to God's Covenant, heals the twisting of the world.

This twisting—which, it must be said, occurs first and foremost in the scientific cities—not only sullies the world with sin, but it darkens the world's theophanic capacity, debilitating Creation's ability to reveal God to us and making obscure that most ancient source of Revelation Paul spoke of as displaying God's eternal power and divine nature since the beginning (see Rom. 1:20). Here we would do well to remember Aquinas's warning that "errors about creatures ... lead one astray from the truth of faith."

In the words of Hans Urs von Balthasar, this twisting takes the form of a "sick blindness" that erases God by erasing Creation, for it "arises from regarding reality as raising no questions, being 'just there.'" This is the blindness of materialism and the technological paradigm that has dominated the West over the last five centuries. This is the blindness that undermines religious faith by eliminating the perception of its conditions of possibility. This is the blindness that diabolically divorces the physical from the metaphysical, the body from the soul, the empirical from the corporeal, the individual from the community, the human from the natural world, and nature from God. This is the blindness that gives rise to deism, by which some demiurge may have made the universe but is not present in it—a Great Architect in the sky, perhaps watching from his heights like the Olympian gods of old, but not interfering.

How clearly this image appears in the distinctly modern works of Hieronymus Bosch, for example, with Christ set in the clouds, watching almost helplessly as demons drag the haywain of earthly vanity into Hell. How different from this late medieval fresco on the outer wall of the church of San Giacomo, in Northern Italy, tucked beneath the Dolomites of Val Gardena: a massive Christ figure, His wounds still bleeding, supplies rivulets of blood to all the members of the community, each performing their daily tasks, though pestered by diminutive demons.

IV. Community and the Covenant

The question of the natural world has little to do with environmentalism or sustainability but rather with the indwelling of God in the world, His self-revelation through the works of His hand, faith in the effectiveness of His sacraments and miracles, and the loving compassion we ought to have toward our fellow creatures, who are, through no sin of their own, companions on the pilgrimage through this valley of tears.

Environmentalism and sustainability are scientific abstractions that lie on the surface of reality and seek only to preserve the extrinsic value of things we no longer know how to love, and yet what they strive after is to be found most originally and most visibly where the relationships within God's Covenant are most fully realized. It should come as no surprise that many of Europe's ancient monasteries are hailed as some of the first examples of self-sufficiency and sustainability and whose lands are now valued as "hotspots of biodiversity" of great interest for conservation.

Love for Creation, for one's home, is never opposed to the supernatural call to train one's eyes on Heaven. It is not despite this world that we must seek our celestial homeland but through it and *with* it, for Creation "has been groaning in labor pains until now," waiting "with eager longing for the revealing of the children of God" (Rom. 8:22, 19). However, this Covenant is not opposed to the use of animals and nature for our needs but elevates those uses beyond mere utility, through love into covenant.

In a letter to Emile Bernard, Vincent Van Gogh rebuked his friend for failing to see the rich Christian symbolism of Rembrandt's *Slaughtered Ox*. Though it shows no more than a skinned carcass, it invokes the feast held for the prodigal son as well as Christ crucified, offering His flesh as life-giving food for prodigal humanity. To be insensitive to the sacrifices that are the source of our very life is to stifle one's soul and damage the beloved community. Cicero observed in *On Duties* that "all men detest ingratitude and look upon the sin of it as a wrong committed against themselves also, because it discourages generosity; and they regard the ingrate as the common foe of all the poor." Similarly, we all suffer the effects of the generalized ingratitude toward the creatures and places by which our Redeemer makes our lives possible.

Modern and postmodern conceptions of nature are caught in a rivalry between "anthropocentric" and "biocentric" positions and instrumental versus intrinsic values. Though containing fragments of truth, both are blind to the Covenant of Creation we have been born into and are called to fulfill. We must go beyond these and other terminology arising from dualistic views of Creation, such as "ecosystem" and "the environment," whenever possible. Instead of such abstract notions that disembody and disconnect us from each other and from reality, Wendell Berry reminds us that real names are those of the particular "rivers and valleys; creeks, ridges, and mountains; towns and cities; lakes, woodlands, lanes, roads, creatures, and people." Berry insists that we will only be able to preserve the places where there are communities of people that love them and care for them; and that we cannot love what we do not know and do not call by its right name.

V. The Richness of the Covenant

On the ecological level, it is only quantitatively better to "buy local," but, for those who are attuned to it, there is a deeper metaphysical reality in the bonds of community actualized at the local farmers' market. The local is vital because it is only locally that one can form true—incarnate—relationships with the people and other creatures we are bound to. The local, even in the midst of poverty, is the storehouse of true ontological wealth, namely, the "richness in the relations that are integral to man's original meaning," as David L. Schindler has put it.

This conception of wealth implies the relative importance of some minimum of quantitative wealth and is not at all juxtaposed to it, but it also helps us see more clearly the primary importance of non-quantifiable values and obliges us to see reality differently by starting from the ontological level. Ontological wealth is diminished by economies of scale. Ontological wealth is the reason artisanal and handmade goods are better and also worth more at market. It describes the pre-rational perception of the authentic, genuine, and real that undercuts the utilitarian calculus of modernity.

This explains why people will buy jeans with holes in them and why homeware industrially produced in Indonesia can make you feel warm and fuzzy when sold under a brand name like "Threshold" if it is printed in an antique typeset along with a logo of a turn-of-the-century skeleton key. These modern simulacra can only mimic the trappings of true community and the ontological bonds that make us human.

Both private life and public life gravitate toward exploitation, competition, and insatiability, but the disciplines of community are what knit them together. Community happens when people depend on one another, but in a world of social media, big-box stores, and one-day shipping, we must choose to make ourselves both dependent on and responsible for our communities and our landscapes, trusting that others will be attracted to this commitment to the real.

Christian civilization is founded on the constitutive relationality that lies at the ontological core of the human person. Failing to understand that "constitutive openness to the other is a primordial fact" leads to a notion of autonomy that posits community as secondary, exterior, manipulable, and ultimately optional. Christian communities, true manifestations of the Universal Church, cannot be founded on a contractual logic but only on love for the ontological reality of our creaturely nature and the designs of Providence. Every attempt to "build community" must privilege this primordial awareness of the giftedness of our relationality and the receptivity necessary to be formed by it, for in these bonds we learn what it means to be creatures of a loving Father, we strengthen our spiritual ties to reality, and we "proclaim the good news to the whole creation."

The Poetics of Place

James Matthew Wilson

In one of Samuel Taylor Coleridge's finest poems, "Frost at Midnight," we encounter what might be called *the* classic romantic lesson in verse-craft as a kind of soul-craft. Coleridge describes the silent house on a chill night, while his "cradled infant slumbers peacefully" at his side. The "strange / And extreme silentness" of the evening leads him to meditate on his own childhood, the present moment, and the future he dreams of for his son, Hartley.

As he thinks with joy of "Sea, hill, and wood" and the "numberless goings on of life" in the village nearby, he finds that it contrasts painfully with one setting of his own childhood, that of Christ's Hospital school, in London, where he was educated and spent most of his youth. He was:

> reared
> In the great city, pent 'mid cloisters dim,
> And saw nought lovely but the sky and stars.

Such an urban education taught him the learning of books and the awe or fear of the "stern preceptor's face," but it was on the whole an education in *superstition*, where he learned to see a fluttering ash on the grate of the fireplace (a "stranger") as a sign that a visitor will soon arrive. In contrast, young Hartley will "wander like a breeze / By lakes and sandy shores," and the "eternal language, which thy God / Utters," through created nature, the communications of the "Great universal Teacher," will inform Hartley's soul, giving him a sweeter self and a happier life than Coleridge had ever known.

We find here much that the discerning reader will want to question. The beauty of the natural world indeed is formative of and salutary for the self; being "pent" in a great city will indeed lead one to develop a character more guarded and aggressive. These are not mere romantic prejudices but the evidences given by every civilization dating back to ancient Rome, where the farmer-soldier was thought the ideal citizen and the Georgic poetic mode of Virgil was thought the most perceptive of the true nature of the world. Modern scientific observation and ancient truisms are alike in this judgment.

And yet Coleridge's stridency overplays this truth. Cities can be—cities usually are—places that form the soul in a salutary manner much as the countryside does, and both country and city play a role in the building up of a good civilization. Further, while the natural world as created has far more to teach us of the nature of God than many modern minds are prepared to credit, Coleridge seems to conflate the city with the intellectual life and its "swimming" (that is to say, day-dreaming and distracted) book learning. He thus suggests a cleavage between the teachings of nature and those of formal literary education that seems to deprecate the latter.

Coleridge, in brief, makes it easy for us to dismiss the theme of his poem as the mere sentimentalism for which the romantics are well known. At the heart of much of the romantic movement's spirit, alas, is the fear that the advance of the new learning, of man's mechanical conquest of nature, has disenchanted the world and left no room of the transcendent aspirations of the soul. As odd as it sounds, for instance, Sir Issac Newton's study in optics was feared to have robbed the lovely rainbow of its myth and magic. The common romantic response, as found for instance in John Keats's "Ode to Psyche," was to make the poetic imagination a pastoral place of refuge. Poetry came to be conceived as a source of consolation, a cloistered temple for spirit, morality, imagination, and feeling, that specifically stood apart from the amoral, desolate, and mutable world as a whole. The world was, again, feared to be what Thomas Hobbes had told us it was more than a century earlier: a realm knowable purely in terms of mechanics—of matter and matter's motions—from which the very language of soul and spirit must be banished as harmful superstition.

As unsatisfactory as this romantic theory must be—and such a separation of truth from goodness, "fact" from "value," seems indeed a pathetic theory capable of convincing no one for long—Coleridge's overall vision should compel us. The romantic movement was often called the "romantic revival," and one of the things it sought to revive was a fuller vision of reality than the crude materialism and mechanism that had come to predominate since the age of Hobbes and Descartes. This is what Coleridge gives to us here in his limpid, meditative blank verse: a scene, indeed a drama, where the mind enters into the particulars of the world and discovers the eternal within the ephemeral, the absolute within the contingent, the spirit within the material. In this, he reunites his modern reader with the great insights of classical civilization, especially those of Plato and Aristotle, which held that the mind's path toward truth entailed a descent into the particular and an ascent within the particular to the universal.

Just as the romantics exaggerated the strength of the senti‑ments to protect our moral beings from a disenchanted truth, the romantics are also thought of as having exaggerated the role of the poet as sage and the poetic as a source of revelation. But in this, too, they were chiefly reviving (with the occasional disfiguring difference) classical thought with its celebration of verse‑making as an inspired way of knowing the world.

In this belief, classical civilization and the romantic movement were one and, to my mind, in the right. What they both encour‑age us to think is that there are properties or aspects of poetry, of the poem in itself, that are revelatory of the nature of reality more generally. To form oneself as in some sense a poet has, analogously, lessons for how we ought to form our souls. In both these realms, that of the poem and that of the poet, we discover that it is only by means of the particular that we can know the universal, that the "local" and the material is the place where we come into contact with the absolute and the spiritual.

Poems are made of those minute surds of metrical feet, and yet through these almost insignificant and unintelligible elements, whole patterns of order and meaning emerge. St. Augustine most famously observed that metrical numbers were temporal expres‑sions of the eternal numbers of the divine order. Plato found in the rhythms of verse a means for the mind to perceive the order of the cosmos. Poetry asks of the poet and the reader of the poem alike an entrance into the imaginable, existent particulars of thought and the world and, without ever leaving them behind, leads us to the gates of being, to the unchanging and essential reality of things. In doing this, poems help teach us how to be human.

The philosopher Martin Heidegger once enjoined human beings to "dwell poetically." I do not think his account of what that meant was the best one, but the phrase itself has always struck me as worth keeping. The practice of poetry and the nature of the poem both have something to teach us about the properly lived human life. In this sense, Coleridge was correct to make a poem about the "secret ministry" that the particulars of verse and nature perform for us. In this sense, the study of poetry is at once a way of knowing—a philosophical activity as Aristotle and Plato variously suggest—and, finally, a humanizing activity. It allows us to be formed through the contemplation of truth in all its elevation and abstraction without ever leaving our particular, immanent condition behind.

The great literary critic W. K. Wimsatt once argued that poems are examples of the "Concrete Universal." Some critics praise poetry as the representation of generals and universals; others praise it for its minute perceptions of the particular. These claims contradict each other, but when taken together, they are correct. Wimsatt writes,

> Whether or not one believes in universals, one may see the persistence in literary criticism of a theory that poetry presents the concrete and the universal, or the individual and the universal, or an object which in a mysterious and special way is both highly general and highly particular. The doctrine is implicit in Aristotle's two statements that poetry imitates action and that poetry tends to express the universal. It is implicit again at the end of the classic period in the mystic doctrine of Plotinus, who in his later writing ... arrives at the view that the artist by a kind of bypass of the inferior natural productions of the world soul reaches straight to the forms that light behind the divine intelligence.

One of the classic expressions of this union of the concrete and the universal appears in Theseus's mocking, incredulous speech near the end of Shakespeare's *A Midsummer Night's Dream*. Hearing the strange tales of the young lovers, he replies,

> More strange than true: I never may believe
> These antique fables, nor these fairy toys.
> Lovers and madmen have such seething brains,
> Such shaping fantasies, that apprehend
> More than cool reason ever comprehends.
> The lunatic, the lover, and the poet
> Are of imagination all compact:
> One sees more devils than vast hell can hold,
> That is, the madman: the lover, all as frantic,
> Sees Helen's beauty in a brow of Egypt:
> The poet's eye, in fine frenzy rolling,
> Doth glance from heaven to earth, from earth to heaven;
> And as imagination bodies forth
> The forms of things unknown, the poet's pen
> Turns them to shapes and gives to airy nothing
> A local habitation and a name.
> Such tricks hath strong imagination,
> That if it would but apprehend some joy,
> It comprehends some bringer of that joy;
> Or in the night, imagining some fear,
> How easy is a bush supposed a bear!

Theseus is not impressed by the poets' "seething brains." Just as the lover sees a face of modest beauty and, in his enthusiasm, takes it for "Helen"; just as those afraid at night suppose a clump of bushes to be a bear; so is it that poets "glance from heaven to earth, from earth to heaven" and give "to airy nothing / A local habitation and a name." That is to say, the poet thinks he perceives all things, chases the essences of things, and confines those evasive generalities into particulars embodied and localized. For Theseus, this is the opposite of good sense, but indeed it is in just this "fine frenzy rolling" that poetry takes the supremely intelligible but abstract and draws it into a form that we can know by way of our native faculty, the imagination. And nothing, as Aristotle most famously argued, *nothing* comes into our intellect except by way of the imagination. Poetry, *pace* Theseus's ironic treatment, is not an idle engine of nonsense but the means by which we make sense of the world by way of the senses—and it is this for just the reason Theseus mentions in the play. Poetry incarnates the universal *logos* of things and allows us to perceive it.

As Coleridge's "Frost at Midnight" exemplifies, poets have often thought of the particulars of the natural world as the clearest sign that poetry initiates us into the particular so that we might also be attuned to the universal. Coleridge, as a faithful romantic, presumes that this can only happen in pastoral places and that the outcome will always be salutary. Robert Frost, in some of his poems, undermines such confidence. "The Need for Being Versed in Country Things," for instance, takes us into nature's "secret ministry" only to argue that it has only its own indifference to share with us. For us, the sight of a burned-out farmhouse evokes a sad sigh, but as for the birds: "For them there was really nothing sad." In his sonnet "Design," Frost entertains the possibility that nature's ministry is a dark one and has only an order of eerie cruelty to share with us, "If design govern in a thing so small." In such poems, a deep cleavage between the human, intelligible world and nature's wild, unintelligible one is the only lesson the latter has to share.

The balance of Frost's poems, however, chastens the romantic hope in nature but finally affirms it. Two early poems, "Mending Wall" and "The Wood-Pile," are exemplary in this regard. The first suggests that a cautious, even superstitious, obedience to the natural order of things is our one stay against confusion. Just as two farmers repair the stone wall that divides their property, so the poet must manage the iambic stones of pentameter verse, if what order there is in the world is to be perceived, maintained, and lived within. The second suggests that the life of such poetic discipline rarely bequeaths us the kinds of epiphany that Coleridge proposes but does allow us to know the world better and to build up an intelligible order within it. Other poems, including "A Fountain, a Bottle, a Donkey's Ears and Some Books" and "Maple," break down the tension between the natural and the human and show human beings to be part of the nature they contemplate. Frost's character as a "regional poet," one committed to knowing the terrain of his adopted home of New England, is not incidental to all of this. A commitment to knowing the particular place is the one path by which things writ large can come to be understood, but such a knowledge of the universal has also the effect of grounding us ever more deeply in the particular.

Wendell Berry and Richard Wilbur are perhaps the two poets of the last half century best known for a commitment to giving names to a particular "habitat" for the sake of understanding it and the whole of reality more deeply. But I want to propose that this is a lesson of every kind of poem, explicitly regional in attentions or otherwise. To "dwell poetically" is to refuse the much-maligned modern tendency to strip the world of its "enchantment," meaning its intelligible significance, and to view it as a mere pile of dust awaiting formation under the power of the human will. It is also to refuse the equally maligned modern tendency to a merely rationalistic abstraction. Human reason by nature begins on the ground of the particular and rises toward the abstract. It goes amiss when this "rise" becomes a departure from the particular or the reduction of reality to a few abstract, usually quantifiable, aspects. Poems remind us of the coexistence of the particular and the universal. The macrocosm appears symbolically in the microcosm; the absolute subsists and is most fully itself when incarnate with a "local habitation and a name."

Poets have no choice but to remember such claims, because poetry is a measured order of words in which the most minute and refined play an irreducible role in the realization of a rhythmic, intellectual whole that is far greater than the sum of its parts—and in which every part may be saturated in meaning. Human beings in general often do forget these claims. This is one reason that poets have historically played a distinctive role in every civilization: classical, romantic, and modern. Poems in themselves resist abstraction and disenchantment. Poems provide a mode of contemplation for the writer and the reader alike to see the world whole by adhering most closely and faithfully to what John Crowe Ransom calls the particular "local texture" of things. Poems constitute a particularized order of words and remind us of the order that transcends us, and they do so refusing ever to surrender form for content or content for mere form, the particular for the universal or the universal for the particular. To dwell poetically is therefore to be faithful to the least aspect of the world and also to know that that smallest of things contains in some sense a ray of the whole. This is what another romantic poet, William Blake, meant when he enjoined us all

> To see a World in a Grain of Sand
> And a Heaven in a Wild Flower
> Hold Infinity in the palm of your hand
> And Eternity in an hour.

Afterword

How to Change the World

Michael Warren Davis

So now you've read the book. You've heard all the arguments—economic, political, historical, etc.—and you don't disagree with a single word. How could you?

This has always been the problem with distributism, or localism, or whatever you want to call it. It is (literally) too obvious.

After all, what are we actually saying? That small businesses are better than big businesses. That independent farmers are better than agribusiness. That local government does a better job of providing for the common good than federal and even state governments. We want big families on a bit of land, at least enough to grow strong and free. We want men to have good jobs making useful, beautiful things. We want women who know true independence from corporate masters, emancipation from wage-slavery. We want our children to grow wise, not merely clever; pious, not merely obedient.

Simply put, we want what most Americans took for granted for most of our nation's history.

Localism

This isn't a pipe dream. It's not some sort of highfalutin theory. It's not even a theory. It's just ... normal.

So why are "serious" thinkers so quick to dismiss localism? To a large extent, it's the media. News corporations have a massive financial incentive to cast every economic, political, or cultural problem as a national problem with a national solution. This in turn gives federal politicians an excuse to collect power in their own hands. These political elites also accept billions of dollars a year from multi-national corporations to stamp out potential competitors, especially small businessmen. A mom-and-pop drugstore is a bigger threat to Walgreens than CVS or Rite Aid. Even the intelligentsia (universities, think-tanks, and the like) are in on the scam. They earn their keep by trading in abstract ideologies. They have to make our problems seem more complicated than they really are. They need us to buy into meaningless concepts like Marxism and capitalism for the same reason companies use terms like "brand awareness" and "corporate culture."

But the blame also lies, in no small part, with ourselves.

Here's the thing about localism: it's easy in theory but hard in practice. All you have to do is carefully budget your time and money so you can patronize local businesses rather than ordering everything through Amazon and Walmart. Well, all right. But who among us feels like he's just wasting gobs of time and money? And where am I even supposed to find an "independent retailer" that sells clothes, for instance? There's a thrift store a few towns over; do I have to do all my shopping there? And even if our family could make this work, how many millions of people would have to do the same before we really made a difference?

These aren't excuses. These are real, legitimate concerns.

Ideology, meanwhile, is just the opposite. It's hard in theory but easy in practice. And regardless of which ideology we're talking about, the practice is always the same: blame someone else. If you're a capitalist, blame the tax-happy politicians. If you're a communist, blame the corporate fat-cats. Either way, *you're* not part of the problem. You're not even part of the solution. You're simply a victim—a victim of "the system."

Localists know there are no systems, only people. And people are selfish. Yes, it seems like the most selfish among us do very well in business and government. But how did they rise so high? That's easy: we put them there. We voted for them. We bought their merchandise. And why? Because they promised to sell us happiness, to sign a better world into law (better for *us*, anyway; let them lock up the other party and throw away the key as far as we're concerned). In other words, they played off our selfishness.

Chesterton believed that, throughout all time, and in every country in the world, this would always be true: "What is wrong with the world is the devil, and what is right with the world is God." He was right, of course. And no executive order can ban temptation. No supercenter, however super, sells virtue in a can. We—the little guys; you and me—have to make that choice for ourselves. We have to make it every day when we get out of bed in the morning and renew it a thousand times before we lie back down to sleep.

This is the only way to change the world—at least for the better. Joseph Stalin and Jeff Bezos harnessed the power of Big Government and Big Business to make the world a worse place to live; Jesus Christ made it better by touching hearts and minds. Christianity was, if nothing else, a moral revolution. And that's what we need today.

I think C. S. Lewis put it best:

> If you read history, you will find that the Christians who did most for the present world were just those who thought

most of the next. The Apostles themselves, who set on foot the conversion of the Roman Empire, the great men who built up the Middle Ages, the English Evangelicals who abolished the Slave Trade, all left their mark on Earth, precisely because their minds were occupied with Heaven.

It is since Christians have largely ceased to think of the other world that they have become so ineffective in this. Aim at Heaven and you will get earth "thrown in": aim at earth and you will get neither.

Whether you profess the Christian faith or not, you know how that carpenter from Nazareth turned the world upside-down by telling men to love God with all their hearts, love their neighbor as themselves, love their enemies, and pray for those who persecute them.

Selfishness is what's wrong with the world, and love is what's good. And love demands sacrifice. That's true for love of neighbor, and it's true for love of self (see "delayed gratification"). As long as we're content to keep screwing our neighbor so we can pleasure ourselves, nothing will change. But if we can learn or re-learn how to love — not because it's easy, or expedient, but because it's the right thing to do — then we can change the world.

About the Contributors

DALE AHLQUIST is president of the Society of Gilbert Keith Chesterton and of the Chesterton Schools Network.

MAX BECHER is an independent farmer, essayist, and speaker. He is also the founder of the *Catholic Agrarian*.

Allan C. Carlson is the John A. Howard Distinguished Fellow for Family and Religious Studies at the International Organization for the Family and a senior editor of *Touchstone: A Journal of Mere Christianity*.

CHRISTOPHER CHECK is the president of Catholic Answers.

DAVID W. COONEY is founder and editor of *Practical Distributism*.

CHARLES A. COULOMBE is a historian and scholar at the International Theological Institute. He is the author, most recently, of *Blessed Charles of Austria: A Holy Emperor and His Legacy* (TAN Books, 2020).

JASON CRAIG is editor of *Those Catholic Men* and *Sword&Spade* magazine. He runs a small grade-A dairy with his family, and he hosts retreats and workshops through St. Joseph's Farm.

Anthony Esolen is Distinguished Professor of Humanities at Thales College. He is the author, most recently, of *The Lies of Our Time* (Sophia Institute Press, 2023).

William Edmund Fahey III is president of the Thomas More College of Liberal Arts.

Sean Fitzpatrick serves on the faculty of Gregory the Great Academy.

Matthew Giambrone is founder and editor of *Hearth & Field*.

Ryan Hanning is professor of Theology and Catholic Studies at the University of Mary Liffrig School of Education and the Franciscan University of Steubenville Catechetical Institute. He is also an active homesteader.

John Kanu is founder and director of the Sierra Leone Chesterton Center.

Chuck Marohn is founder and president of Strong Towns. He is also an experienced land-use planner and civil engineer.

Joseph Pearce is visiting professor of literature at Ave Maria University and a visiting chair of Catholic studies at the Thomas More College of Liberal Arts. He is the author, most recently, of *The Good, the Bad, and the Beautiful* (Ignatius Press, 2023).

Fr. Michael Rennier is a priest of the Archdiocese of St. Louis and web editor of *Dappled Things*.

About the Contributors

E. WESLEY REYNOLDS III is director of the Wilbur Fellows Program at the Russell Kirk Center and teaches history at Northwood University. He is the author of *Coffeehouse Culture in the Atlantic World, 1650–1789* (Bloomsbury Academic, 2022).

CARMEL RICHARDSON is a wife, mother, and Tennessean. She is a columnist and contributing editor at *The American Conservative*.

MARCO RUBIO is a United States senator representing Florida. He is the author, most recently, of *Decades of Decadence: How Our Spoiled Elites Blew America's Inheritance of Liberty, Security, and Prosperity* (Broadside Books, 2023).

MARCO SERMARINI is a criminal lawyer and the founder of Scuola Libera Gilbert Keith Chesterton in San Benedetto del Tronto, Le Marche, Italy.

THOMAS STORCK has taught history at Christendom College and philosophy at Mount Aloysius College and serves on the editorial board of *The Chesterton Review*. He is the author, most recently, of *The Prosperity Gospel: How Greed and Bad Philosophy Distorted Christ's Teachings* (TAN Books, 2023).

MICHAEL DOMINIC TAYLOR is teaching fellow at the Thomas More College of Liberal Arts and received the Expanded Reason Award from the Joseph Ratzinger Foundation in 2021. He is the author of *The Foundations of Nature: Metaphysics of Gift for an Integral Ecological Ethic* (Cascade Books, 2020).

JAMES MATTHEW is Wilson Cullen Foundation Chair in English at the University of St. Thomas–Houston, where he co-founded the

Master's in Fine Arts program in creative writing. The winner of the 2017 Hiett Prize from the Dallas Institute of Humanities and Culture, Wilson also serves as poet-in-residence of the Benedict XVI Institute for Sacred Music and Divine Worship and poetry editor of *Modern Age magazine*.

MICHAEL WARREN DAVIS is contributing editor for *The American Conservative* and the author, most recently, of *After Christendom* (Sophia Institute Press, 2024).

Sophia Institute

Sophia Institute is a nonprofit institution that seeks to nurture the spiritual, moral, and cultural life of souls and to spread the gospel of Christ in conformity with the authentic teachings of the Roman Catholic Church.

Sophia Institute Press fulfills this mission by offering translations, reprints, and new publications that afford readers a rich source of the enduring wisdom of mankind.

Sophia Institute also operates the popular online resource CatholicExchange.com. *Catholic Exchange* provides world news from a Catholic perspective as well as daily devotionals and articles that will help readers to grow in holiness and live a life consistent with the teachings of the Church.

In 2013, Sophia Institute launched Sophia Institute for Teachers to renew and rebuild Catholic culture through service to Catholic education. With the goal of nurturing the spiritual, moral, and cultural life of souls, and an abiding respect for the role and work of teachers, we strive to provide materials and programs that are at once enlightening to the mind and ennobling to the heart; faithful and complete, as well as useful and practical.

Sophia Institute gratefully recognizes the Solidarity Association for preserving and encouraging the growth of our apostolate over the course of many years. Without their generous and timely support, this book would not be in your hands.

www.SophiaInstitute.com
www.CatholicExchange.com
www.SophiaInstituteforTeachers.org

Sophia Institute Press is a registered trademark of Sophia Institute.
Sophia Institute is a tax-exempt institution as defined by the
Internal Revenue Code, Section 501(c)(3). Tax ID 22-2548708.